THE

MOTHER'S NEW READER,

OR

CHILD'S INSTRUCTOR;

CONTAINING

EASY LESSONS FOR CHILDREN,

ON FAMILIAR SUBJECTS,

IN LANGUAGE SUITED TO THEIR CAPACITIES.

A NEW EDITION, REVISED AND IMPROVED

BY R. D. MARSH,

LATE TEACHER IN THE NEW YORK GRAMMAR SCHOOL.

NEW YORK:

RICHARD MARSH, 374 PEARL STREET,

PUBLISHER, BOOKSELLER, AND BLANK-BOOK MANUFACTURER.

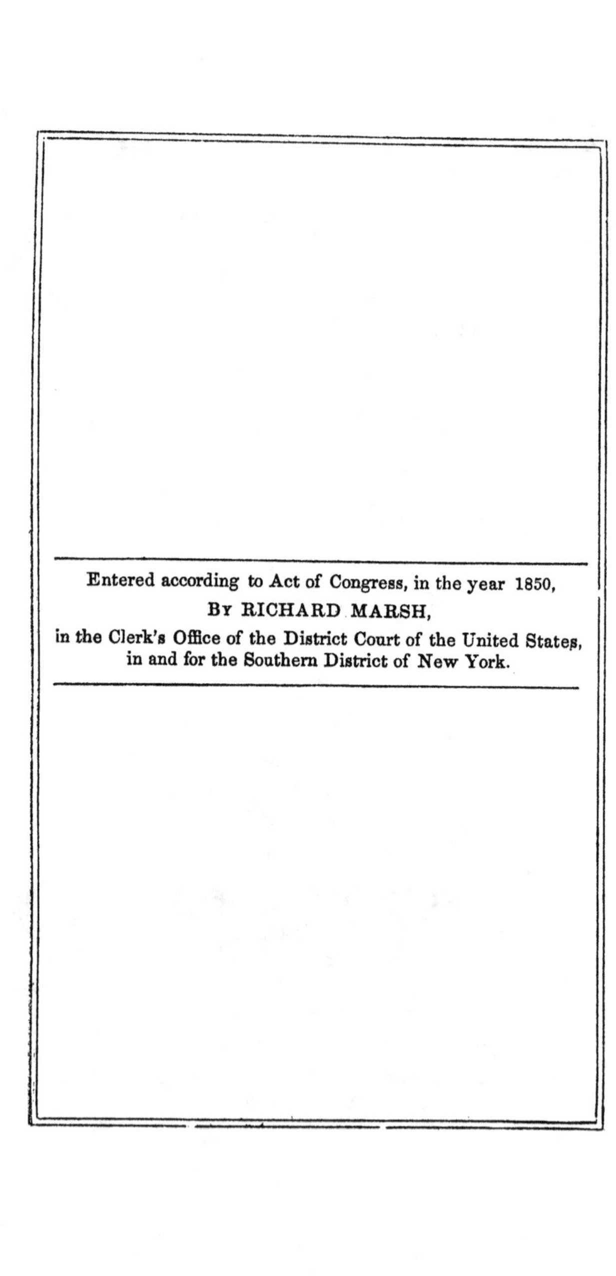

Ale	Bale	Cale	Dale
Ear	Fear	Gear	Hear
Ice	Joist	Kine	Line
Mine	Nine	Ore	Pore
Quail	Sail	Rail	Vail
Wolf	Wax	Year	Zeal

Ask	mask.	Ush	Mush.
Buff	muff.	Loss	moss.
Rest	west.	Fire	fill.
Sire	sill.	Flip	flow.
Slip	slow.	Act	fact.

Are you blind?
Come here, Dog.
Eat your Fish.
Go and hunt.
It was Jack.
Kite and Lark.
Mouse and Nag.
Ox and Pig.
Quails will run.
Spin your Top.
Use the Vine.
Where are X Y & Z?

Let this be your plan,
Learn all that you can.

Ant.
Bug.
Cup.
Doe.
Egg.
Fan.
Gun.
Hen.
Ink.
Jug.
Key.
Lark.
Man.
Nail.
Owl.
Pig.
Quill.
Ruff.
Sun.
Tree.
Urn.
Vane.
Wolf.
Yam.

CHAPTER II. SECOND.

1. Now George, you know all the letters.
Now you must learn to spell and read.
A good boy will sit still, and mind his book.

2. Knife, fork, spoon, plate, dish, cup, bowl, mug, jug, pot, pan, tub, chair, ta-ble, bench bed, box, desk, fire, wood, shov-el, tongs, bel-lows.

3. What is your name? My name is George. How old are you? Four years old. Do you go to school? Yes sir. Can you spell? Yes sir, a little.

4. Bread, but-ter, cheese, meat, pud-ding, pie, cake, beef, pork, veal, soup, sauce, salt, pep-per, gra-vy, mus-tard, su-gar, ho-ney, jel-ly, car-rot.

5. George, can you count twenty? Yes sir, One, two, three, four, five, six, sev-en, eight, nine, ten, e-le-ven, twelve, thir-teen, four-teen, fif-teen, six-teen, sev-en-teen, eigh-teen, nine-teen, twen-ty.

6. Now George, you can count Twenty, you must keep your place yourself, and learn to spell the two following lessons.

7. Ab eb ib ob ub, ac ec ic oc uc.
Ad ed id od ud, af ef if of uf.
Ag eg ig og ug, ak ek ik ok uk.
Ar er ir or ur, ap ep ip op up.

8. Ba be bi bo bu by, ca ce ci co cu cy.
Da de di do du dy, fa fe fi fo fu fy.
Ha he hi ho hu hy, ja je ji jo ju jy.
Na ne ni no nu ny, sa se si so su sy.

CHAPTER III. THIRD.

1. George, do you know how many Letters there are? Yes sir. Twenty-six. Can you spell the letters? Yes sir. A, be, ce, de, E, ef, je, aitch, I, ja, ka, el, em, en, O, pe, cu, ar, es, te, U, ve, double-you, ex, Y, zed.

2. George, do you know how many vow-els there are? Yes sir. Six: a, e, i, o, u, y, are vow-els; and b, c, d, f, g, h, j, k, l, m, n, p, q, r, s, t, v, w, x, z, are con-so-nants. There are six vow-els, and twen-ty con-so-nants.

3. Ace age ale, and ape ask, all awe law.
Eke eve cell, elk end est.
Ice ile ire, ind ilk ist.
Ode ope ore, oft ord oct.
Ude une use, uft ust urn.

4. George, do you know who made you? Yes sir: God made me, and takes care of me. He loves good boys and good girls, and we must love him. God is very good to take care of us.

5. Make, bake, cake, band, hand, land, ball,
Call, beer, dear, fear, bend, dent, pent.

Bind, find, mind, bilk, milk, silk.
Gore, pore, torn, corn, horn, morn.
Cure, sure, pure, burk, lurk, turk.

6. When you go to bed, you should pray to God; and when you get up, do the same. If you have done a fault, confess it, and take care to do so no more.

7. Bane, cane, mane, ban, can, man, halt, malt, salt.
Fere, here, mere, fer, her, mer.
Fine, pine, wine, fin, pin, win.
Cote, note, rote, cot, not, rot.
Cube, rube, tube, cub, rub, tub.

Please to give me my hat. Please to give me a drink. Please to let me go out. Where is my whip? Where is my horse?

Here is your horse, you may ride him to town,
To buy you a book, and your sis-ter a gown.

Head, hair, skin, skull, brow, face, eye, ear, cheek, nose, mouth, lip, tongue, tooth, teeth, gums, jaws, chin, neck, throat, breast, heart, shoul-der, arm, el-bow, wrist, hand, fin-ger, thumb, knee, leg, an-kle, foot, toe.

A good boy and a good girl will get good things. All the boys will love them, and God will bless them. Good boys mind their books.

Li-on leop-ard, ti-ger, ca-mel, bul-lock,

po-ny, mon-key, rab-bit, squir-rel. Bear, ox, calf, horse, swine, pig, mouse, rat, sheep, ram, goat, deer, lamb, fox, hare, el-e-phant.

As the mind of a child is like soft wax, which will take the least stamp you put on it, so let it be your care, who teach, to make the stamp good, that the wax be not hurt. Teach him to love God, and to o-bey his pa-rents.

CHAPTER IV. FOURTH.

1. A good boy will do as he is bid: he will mind his book and try to learn. Who is a good boy? Charles is a good boy; and so is George.

2. If you are a good boy like Charles, and try to learn, you shall have a top. And you may spin your top. Bad boys shall have no tops.

3. If you are good, all the boys will love you and play with you; but if you are not good, the boys will not love you.

4. Here is a nut. Crack this nut for Charles. If you will be good, you shall have nuts to crack. Do you like nuts? Yes sir. Nuts are very good.

5. Here is a plum for you. Who will have this plum? Charles shall have it, for he sits still, and makes no noise. Charles is a good boy.

6. Did you see that boy run? he lost his hat: pick up his hat. Give the poor boy his hat. Here, boy, take your hat.

7. The child fell down and hurt his arm. Poor child, do not cry; do not cry; you shall have some cake. Give the child some cake.

8. Eagle, hawk owl, crow, crane, dove, pi-ge-on

hen, chick-en, gan-der, goose, gos-ling, tur-key, pea-cock, phea-sant, black-bird, par-rot, spar-row, ro-bin, swal-low, gold-finch, mag-pie.

CHAPTER V. FIFTH.

1. Charles is now four years old: he goes to school and learns to read. Charles is a good boy. Who is a good girl? Ann is a good girl.

2. Ann goes to school and learns to read. Good girls mind their books. Good girls and good boys shall have good things.

3. Charles shall have a kite; and he may fly his kite. Ann shall have a doll; and she may dress her doll. Charles and Ann may go in the yard and play.

4. Frank is a good boy: he loves his school and learns to read. He can spell hard words, and is head of his class. Frank shall have a new hat, and new shoes, and go to the fair.

5. Who will go to the fair and buy fine things? All good girls and good boys, who do as they are bid, shall go to the fair and buy fine things.

6. Jane is a good girl: she does as she is bid: her face and hands are clean, and she goes to school. Jane shall have a new frock, and a new fan, and red shoes.

7. Frank and Jane shall have a coach; and they shall ride in a coach. Ann, and Jane, and Frank, and Charles, shall have nuts, and cakes, and pies, and all good things.

CHAPTER VI. SIXTH.

1. The sun is up: get out of bed: come down stairs: wash your face: comb your hair: eat your

breakfast: puss wants her breakfast: poor puss! she cries: she is hungry: give her some breakfast.

2. Now take your book. Learn your task, learn it well. Mind the stops when you read: speak your words plain. Do not tear your book, nor make dog's ears in it. Naughty boys tear books.

3. A cat will scratch: a dog will bark: a hog will squeal: a mouse will squeak: a worm will crawl: an ant will run: a flea will hop: a frog will jump: a bird will fly.

4. Horses haul wood. Cows give milk. Calves make veal. Ships go to sea. Men build ships. Boys learn to sing. Girls learn to dance. Spiders make webs, and bees make honey.

5. Do you like honey? O how sweet! Bees get honey from flowers, and bring it home for good boys. If you learn to read well, you shall have some honey on your bread.

Break-fast, hun-gry, naugh-ty, hor-ses, spi-der, ho-ney, flow-er, din-ner, lit-tle, pud-ding, drow-sy, af-ter, sup-per, al-ways, bro-ther, sis-ter, pa-pa, mam-ma.

CHAPTER VII. SEVENTH.

1. Here is Frank; he is just come home; he has been at school like a good boy: Frank must have some dinner: here is some soup for you: take your spoon and eat. Soup will make little boys grow.

2. Hold your plate, here is some meat: take your knife and fork, and eat a little. Do you want a drink? Take your cup, and drink some milk. Little boys should drink sweet milk.

3. Here is a plum pudding. Frank, do you like

pudding? Give the boy a little. Boys should not eat too much: if they eat too much, they will be dull and drowsy, and will not learn.

4. Now, Frank, you have done your dinner. Sit down here—after dinner sit a while: after supper walk a mile. Sit down, and I will tell you what Charles said one day when he came from school.

5. Charles said he would love his papa and mamma, and always do as he was bid. He would love his brothers and sisters, and would play with them. He would not play with bad boys.

Cheat-ing, pros-per, live-ly, check-ers, mar-bles, Tom-my, dir-ty, ug-ly, pave-ment, peo-ple, ve-ry, some-times, can-not, play-ing, jack-stones, ex-er-cise, chil-dren, an-gry. Be-cause, re-mem-ber.

CHAPTER VIII. EIGHTH.

1. Now, boys, you may go and play. You must not play with bad boys, for they will cheat. You must play fair. Cheating play will never prosper. If you cheat, good boys will not play with you.

2. Do not play too hard: you will hurt the little boys. Be brisk and lively at play; but you must not

be rude. Use no bad words when you play; naughty boys say bad words.

3. What will you play? Will you play hide and whoop? or blind hob, or checkers, or ball? Or will you whip the top, or jump the rope, or shoot marbles? or what will you play?

4. Tommy says he will not play marbles; he calls it a low kind of play. He says the boys who play marbles, get into the dirt, and dirty their hands and their clothes; and you know you look ugly when you are dirty.

5. Here is a top. Can you spin your top? You should not spin your top on the foot pavement, because you will be in the way: people must walk on the foot pavements. Go in the yard, and spin your top there.

6. Can you play ball? here is a ball for you; toss it up. This is a very good ball; I bought it for a very good boy: see how it will bound. Can you catch the ball? Come, let us play.

7. Can you jump the rope? Little girls jump the rope. Girls must play sometimes as well as boys, and they cannot always be playing jack-stones, you know: so they must jump the rope. It is good exercise for them.

8. Children, you must remember, when you are at play, that God sees you all the time; he knows when you are naughty. He hears all you say; and if you say bad words, he will be angry. If you are good when you play, God will love you.

Bil-ly, Bet-sey, preach-er, pa-rents, prais-es, talk-ing, wor-ship, hea-ven, plea-sure, sab-bath, me-mo-ry, doc-trines, bet-ter, ten-der, de-light-ful, be-low, for-get, di vine.

CHAPTER IX. NINTH.

1. Good boys and good girls go to church. Did you go to church? Billy went to church, and so did Betsey. The church is the house of God; and God loves little children when they go to church.

2. When you go to church, you must sit still, and hear what the preacher tells you; he tells you to be good children, and love your parents, and then God will bless you.

3. Did you hear them sing in church? There all the people sing praises to God, and thank him for taking care of us. Once there was a very good man who lived in London: he wrote some very good songs for children; and here is one of them.

4 Lord, how delightful 'tis to see
Young children meet to worship Thee;
At once they sing, at once they pray,
They hear of heaven, and learn the way.

5 I've been to church, and love to go,
'Tis like a little heaven below;
Not for my pleasure and my play,
Will I forget the sabbath-day.

6 O write upon my memory, Lord,
The text, and doctrines of thy word;
That I may break thy laws no more,
But love thee better than before.

7 With thoughts on heaven, and things divine,
O fill this tender heart of mine:
That when at home, or when abroad,
I still may think on Thee, my God.

Giv-eth, mak-eth, touch-eth, fin-ger, glad-ness pierc-ing, se-cret, ac-tions, o-pen, wick-ed, dread-ful, judg-ment, sin-ful, ev-e-ry. A-bove, a-sleep, a-way, Al-migh-ty, com-mit, a-gainst, for-ev-er.

CHAPTER X. TENTH.

1. God is in heaven, and we are on earth: As the heavens are high above the earth, so are his ways above our ways. He giveth light to the sun, and maketh the moon to rise; He toucheth the stars with his finger, and they run their course with gladness.

2. God made the world, and all things that are in the world: He makes us all, and takes care of us, both when we are asleep, and when we are awake. When we go out, he knows all that we do, and when we come in, no door can hide us from him.

3 Almighty God, thy piercing eye
Strikes through the shades of night;
And our most secret actions lie
All open to thy sight.

4 There's not a sin that we commit,
No wicked word we say;
But in thy dreadful book 'tis writ,
Against the judgment day.

5 O God, may I for ever fear,
T' indulge a sinful thought;
Since the great Judge will see and hear,
And write down every fault.

Daz-zle, ea-gle, in-to, beau-ti-ful, ri-ses, hous-es, stee-ples, gild-ed, e-ver, ear-ly, call-ed, Phœ-bus, bur-nish, hunts-man, loos-ed, shep-herd, pla-ced, wretch-ed, ne-ver, evil. Re-tire, Cre-a-tor.

CHAPTER XI. ELEVENTH.

1. How bright the sun is! Can you look at the sun? It will dazzle your eyes. Eagles can look at the sun. If you smoke a piece of glass, and look at the sun through that, it will not dazzle your eyes.

2. When the sun is down, the birds will go to sleep, and little boys should go to bed: and when the sun rises, the birds will wake up and sing: the eagle will soar up into the sky, to gaze at the sun; and the owl will hide from the light.

3. How beautiful is the sun when it rises! It shines on the tops of houses and steeples, and they look as though they were gilded with gold. Did you ever see the sun rise? If you will get up early, you may see it rise. The sun is called Phœbus.

4 Bright Phœbus will rise in the morn,
And burnish the steeples with gold;
Then the huntsman will sound the sweet horn,
And the sheep will be loosed from the fold.

When Phœbus sinks down in the west,
The shepherd takes care of his sheep:
The birds all retire to their rest,
And good little boys go to sleep.

5. The sun is a great fire which makes the world warm. It is a great lamp placed in the sky to give us light. If the sun did not rise, it would be always dark. If the sun should forget to rise, how wretched should we be!

6. Do you know who made the sun? Yes: God made the sun; and he makes it to rise every day. God is very good to make the sun rise for us: He never forgets us one day: and we should never forget him.

7. Remember thy Creator now, in the days of thy

youth, while the evil days come not, nor the years draw nigh, when thou shalt say, "I have no pleasure in them."—While the sun, or the light, or the moon, or the stars are not darkened, nor the clouds return after the rain.

Ri-sing, thun-der, light-ning, far-mer, car-ries, mil-ler, ba-ker, bis-cuit, peach-es, cher-ries, ap-ples, parch-ed, ri-ver, dri-ed, no-thing, thank-ful, clou-dy, wa-ter, show-ers, joy-ful, gras-sy, va-ri-ous, nour-ish, cis-tern, crys-tal, mar-gin. En-rich-ing, al-lay.

CHAPTER XII. TWELFTH.

1. Do you know who makes it rain? I will tell you. God makes it rain. Do you see that dark cloud rising in the west? That cloud will bring thunder and lightning and rain. You need not be afraid. God makes it thunder; and he will not let it hurt you, if you are good.

2. If it did not rain, the grass would not grow, and then the cows would give us no milk. Cows eat grass, and that makes them give milk. Milk, you know, is good for little boys. Bread and milk are good; and so are mush and milk.

3. If it did not rain, the wheat would not grow; and then we should have no bread. The farmer carries wheat to mill; the miller grinds it into flour; and then the baker makes bread of it, and biscuit too.

4. If it did not rain, the trees would not grow; pears grow on trees; peaches grow on trees; cherries grow on trees; and apples grow on trees: if it did not rain, there would be no pears, nor peaches, nor cherries, nor apples.

5. If it did not rain, there would be no water; the

springs, and brooks, and rivers, would all be dried up and then you would have nothing to drink, and we should all die. God is very good to make it rain, and we should all of us be very thankful.

6 God from his cloudy cistern pours
On the parch'd earth enriching showers;
The grove, the garden, and the field,
A thousand joyful blessings yield.

He makes the grassy food arise,
And gives the cattle large supplies:
With herb for man, of various power,
To nourish nature, or to cure.

He bids the crystal fountains flow,
And cheer the valleys as they go:
The flocks and herds their thirst allay,
While lambs upon the margin play.

From pleasant trees which shade the brink,
The lark and linnet light to drink;
Their songs, the lark and linnet raise,
And chide our silence in His praise.

Want-ed, di-ed, o-pen-ed, Har-ry, hol-low, nei-ther ro-sy, ver-dant, hum-ble, glean-er, scat-ter-ed, na-ture, view-ing, kind-ly, boun-te-ous, war-bling, ca-rol, lea-fy, dwel-ling, gol-den. A-way, your-selves, a-bout, ap-pear-ing, dis-port-ing, con-tent, pro-claim-ing, for-sake, se-cure.

CHAPTER XIII. THIRTEENTH.

1. Once Tommy had a little bird; it was a sweet little bird; he put it in a cage, and fed it, and gave it drink; he took good care of it, yet it wanted to get out and fly away: but Tommy would not let it fly away; so the poor thing died in the cage.

2. Once Billy had a bird in a cage, and the bird wanted to get out; so Billy opened the door of the cage, and took it out. Poor bird! said he, I do not want to hurt you: go, fly away to the trees, and find your mamma.

3. Harry, would you keep a poor little bird shut up in a cage? You would not like yourself to be shut up all night, and all day, in a hollow tree: so the poor bird does not like to be shut up in a cage.

4. Now, says Billy, I will tell you what my mamma says about birds: She says that God made the birds, and little boys should not hurt them, nor rob their nests neither. God made them to fly about and sing Can you sing?

5 When the rosy morn appearing,
Paints with gold the verdant lawn:
Bees on banks of thyme disporting,
Sip the sweets, and hail the dawn.
See content the humble gleaner,
Takes the scattered ears that fall;
Nature all her children viewing,
Kindly bounteous, gives to all.

6 Warbling birds, the day proclaiming,
Carol sweet the lively strain;
They forsake their leafy dwelling,
To secure the golden grain.
See content, &c.

CHAPTER XIV. FOURTEENTH.

1. It is a fine thing to talk and read well. Puss can play as well as you, and puss can eat and drink, and she can run as well as you.

2. Puss can climb up trees, and she can catch mice, which is more than you can do. But can puss talk? No. Can puss read? No.

3. Can your dog Tray read? No. Will you teach him? take a pin and point to the words. No, he will not learn, he cannot talk.

4. I never saw a dog or a cat that could learn to read; but boys and girls can learn. If you do not learn, you are not good for half so much as puss.

CHAPTER XV. FIFTEENTH.

1. What o'clock is it? It is twelve o'clock. It is noon. Now where is the sun? The sun is in the south. Turn your face to him. Look at the sun.

2. That way is the south. Always when it is twelve o'clock, and when you look at the sun, your face is to the south, your back is to the north, your left hand is to the east, and your right hand to the west.

3. The sun rises in the east, and sets in the west. Far in the north it is cold weather, and in the south it is warm weather. East, west, north, and south.

4. The wind blows. Which way does the wind blow? Throw up some grass, and that will tell you. The wind blows this way.

5. The wind blows from the north. The north wind is cold, the south wind is warm, the east wind will bring a storm of rain, and the west wind will bring a storm of thunder.

CHAPTER XVI. SIXTEENTH.

1. Come here, Charles, and look at the sun. The sun is in the west. Yes, in a short time it will set. We can look at the sun now, he is not so bright as he was at noon, when he was up high in the sky.

2. See how fine the clouds are! Now the sun goes down very fast. We can see but half of him. Now he is all gone. Good night, sun.

3. Now turn your face to the east. What is that so bright there? Is it fire? No, it is the moon. How large and red it is! The moon is round now, because it is full moon: but it will not be quite so round to-morrow night; it will lose a small piece; and the next night it will lose a piece more; and the next night, a piece more; and so on, till it is like your bow when it is bent.

4. It will not rise till you are gone to bed; and will grow less and less, till, in two weeks, there will be no moon to be seen.

5. Then there will be a new moon, and you will see it when it is near night; it will be crooked and sharp at each end; but it will grow more and more, till, at last, in two weeks' time, it will be a round full moon like this; and you will then see it rise again in the east, as this now does.

Learn-ed, gen-tle-man, look-ed, spec-ta-cles, pa-rents, his-to-ry, prov-ed, chirp-ed, wrap-ped, car-ri-ed, at-tempt, in-quire, bo-dy, con-sti-tutes, wis-dom, block-head, form-ed, ho-nor, es-teem, be-lov-ed, ad mir-ed.

CHAPTER XVII. SEVENTEENTH.

SOMETHING ABOUT TOM THUMB.

1. We are told in the life of Tom Thumb, that he was so small at his birth, that no one thought him worth taking notice of; till a learned gentleman looked at him through a pair of spectacles, and informed his parents that he would be a very little man, and a very great man.

2. And you, who have read the history of Tom Thumb, know that the words of the learned gentleman proved true: for though so very little when a boy, he was so good, and minded his book so well, that he became a very wise and great man.

3. When his father heard that Tom was to be a great man, he took him up on his little finger, and chirped to him, as a boy does to a bird; and his mother wrapped him up in a piece of cotton, put him in a thimble, and carried him about in her warm pocket.

4. The history further informs us, that Tom Thumb became a greater man than his mother; but, before we attempt to prove this, we must inquire what makes a great man.

5. Is it a great head? No. Is it a long leg? No. Is it a big body? No. Is it a great leg? No: but I will tell you what it is: it is a wise head, and a good heart, that constitute a great man.

6. It is wisdom and virtue, and that only, which can make us great and happy. A great brute, or a

great bear, or a great blockhead, may be made by other means.

7. But a great man cannot be formed without wisdom and virtue, which are the only sources of honor and esteem, and will always make us beloved and admired.

Beau-ti-ful, mos-sy, per-fum-ed, o-dor, fair-er, love-ly, rais-eth, shak-eth, roar-ing, des-erts, ter-ri-ble, glo-ri-ous, hea-vens, crea-ture, bright-ness, coun-te-nance, cen-tre.

CHAPTER XVIII. EIGHTEENTH.

1. Come, and I will show you what is beautiful. It is a rose full blown. See how she sits upon her mossy stem, like the queen of all the flowers! the air is perfumed with her odor; she is the delight of every eye.

2. She is beautiful: but there is a fairer than she. He who made the rose, is more beautiful than the

rose: He is all lovely: He is the delight of every heart.

3. I will show you what is strong. The Lion is strong: when he raiseth himself from his den; when he shaketh his mane; when the voice of his roaring is heard, the cattle of the field fly, and the wild beasts of the desert fly and hide themselves, for he is very terrible.

4. The lion is strong; but He who made the lion is stronger than he. He could tear the world to pieces; He could make us die in a moment, and no one could save us out of His hand.

5. I will show you what is glorious. The sun is glorious. When he shineth in the clear sky; when he sitteth on his bright throne in the heavens, and looketh abroad over all the earth; he is the most glorious creature that the eye can behold.

6. The sun is glorious: but He who made the sun is more glorious than he. The eye cannot behold Him, for his brightness is more dazzling than the sun. He seeth in all the dark places, by night as well as by day; and the light of His countenance is over all His works.

7. Who is this that is greater than all things, and what is his name, that my lips may praise him?

8. He is God! who made all things: He sitteth on His throne in the centre, and His breath giveth life to the world. He hath made all things beautiful: but He is more beautiful than they.

9. I will always give thanks unto the Lord; his praise shall ever be in my mouth. My soul shall make her boast in the Lord; the humble shall hear it and be glad. O praise the Lord with me, and let us bless his name always.

Un-der, a-pron, ink-ed, pen-cil, car-pet, gal-loping, hith-er, li-lies, or-an-ges, yel-low, rai-sin, ro-ses, blos-som, wea-ther, cheer-ful, cow-slip, care-less-ly, breech-es, sad-dle, ba-bies, cra-dle, Bet-ty, ham-mer, gin-ger-bread, guin-ea, dol-lar, quar-ter, wo-man, al-ly, some-thing, can-dles, hu-mor-ed, cri-ed, sil-ly, chuck-er, sleep-y, pil-low, co-ver. A-long, re-joice, be-lief.

CHAPTER XIX. NINETEENTH.

1. Papa, where is Charles? Where is the little boy? Ah, here he is, hid under mamma's apron. How do you do, sir? I hope you are very well. See, you have inked your frock: you should take care. Here is a slate and pencil for you. Now sit down and draw a little bird.

2. Charles, what were eyes made for? To see with: and ears to hear with: tongue to talk with: nose to smell with: teeth are to bite with; and legs are to walk with. Come, let us walk to the fields, and see the sheep, and the lambs, and cows, and calves, and birds, and trees.

3. Did you see that horse galloping along? The man rides on the horse. There is a little dog. The dog barks. Do not be afraid, he will not bite you. Come hither, dog. Stroke him, and pat his head: poor dog! Let him lick your hand, he will not bite

you. Come, Charles, let us go home to mamma. Take these flowers, and give them to your little sister.

4. Ink is black. Milk is white. Grass is green. The sky is blue. Fire is red, and Sally's shoes are red. O what fine red shoes! Oranges are yellow. Black, white, green, blue, red, and yellow.

5. Pray give me a raisin. What will you do with it? I want it to eat. Well, here is one. I want two. Well, here they are. I want a great many; I want ten: and here they are. One, two, three, four, five, six, seven, eight, nine, ten. Now what will you do with all these raisins? Give Billy some, and sister Sally.—Good boy!

6. It is winter now; cold winter. There is ice on the river. It hails and snows. Will you run out in the snow? Go, then, and make snow-balls. Pretty snow! how white it is, and how soft it is! bring the snow to the fire: See how it melts! it is all gone now; it has turned to water.

7. When spring comes again, there will be green leaves, and flowers, and daisies, and pinks, and violets, and roses, and warm weather. Come, spring; come, and make the trees blossom, and make the grass grow.

How cheerful, along the gay mead,
The daisy and cowslip appear!
The flocks, as they carelessly feed,
Rejoice in the spring of the year.

8. When Charles is a big boy, he shall have breeches, and a pair of boots; and he shall have a little horse of his own, and a saddle and bridle, and whip, and then he shall ride out with papa.

9. I heard somebody cry just now; I wonder who it was: it was some naughty boy, I fancy. Good boys do not cry—little babies cry. Charles was a little baby

once, and lay in the cradle; but now you are a little boy, and can ride upon a stick.

10. See, here is Betty come from the fair. What has she got? She has got a gun for Charles; and a cane, and a hammer, and some gingerbread: she is very good—thank you, Betty. You must walk with your cane, and shoot with your gun, and eat your gingerbread; but you must not eat it all; give some to sister Sally.

11. Look here, Charles, here is money: what is that yellow piece? This is gold; it is a guinea. Here is a dollar, and half of a dollar, and a quarter of a dollar; and one, two, three, four, five, six pennies. O mamma, give me the pennies.

12. What will you do with the pennies, Charles? Why mamma, there is a poor woman lives in the alley, with four little children, and they are hungry. Their mother is sick, and nobody takes care of them; I will buy something for them to eat. Good boy! take them all.

13. It is night. Betty, bring candles. Look at the moon! O pretty moon! The moon shines for us at night when the sun has gone to bed. Good moon! Once there was a boy who was humored in every thing, and he cried for the moon: That is my moon says he, give me the moon; I will have the moon. He was a silly boy; was he not?

14. The sun is gone to bed; the chickens have gone to bed; the birds have gone to bed; and Charles must go to bed. Poor little boy! he is sleepy. Pull off his shoes. I believe we must carry him up stairs. Lay his little head on the pillow, and cover him up. Good night. Shut your eyes, and go to sleep.

Now I lay me down to sleep,
I pray the Lord my soul to keep,

If I should die before I wake,
I pray the Lord my soul to take.

Sun-day, Mon-day, Tues-day, Wed-nes-day, Thurs-day, Fri-day, Sa-tur-day.—Jan-u-a-ry, Feb-ru-a-ry, A-pril, Ju-ly, Au-gust. Al-ma-nac, e-qual, num-ber, thir-ty, twen-ty, freez-es, fro-zen, slid-ing, skat-ing, drown-ed, grow-ing, long-er, al-most, com-ing, col-or go-ing, fare-well, plea-sant, pay-ing, ro-bin, sum-mer, hot-test, gar-den, suc-kle, mel-ons, fir-ed, shoot-ing, blood-y, flut-ters, sor-ry, fall-ing, ci-der, sto-ries, pic-tures. Christ-mas, bu-sy, do-ing, part-ing, won-der, ho-li-days, her-bage, au-tumn, trea-sures. Sep-tem-ber, Oc-to-ber, No-vem-ber, De-cem-ber, a-lone, a-mong, un-fold.

CHAPTER XX. TWENTIETH.

1. Charles, do you know how many days there are in a week? Yes, seven: Sunday, Monday, Tuesday, Wednesday, Thursday, Friday, Saturday: there are seven days in a week, and four weeks in a month.

2. Charles, how many months are there in one year? Twelve: January, February, March, April, May, June, July, August, September, October, November, December. Twelve months make one year.

3. Charles, the almanac makers say, that each month has not an equal number of days: how many days are in each month?

Thirty days hath September,
April, June, and November;
All the rest have thirty-one,
But February, which alone
Has twenty-eight of Julian time
And every leap-year twenty-nine.

4. January is a very cold month. It snows, and it freezes. There are no leaves on the trees. The milk is frozen, and the river is frozen. All the boys are sliding on the ice. There is a man skating: how fast he goes! I will buy Charles a pair of skates. But you must take care, there is a hole in the ice. If you fall in, you will be drowned.

5. February is cold too; but the days are growing longer, and March will soon come. March is the first month of spring. Now the wind blows hard. It will almost blow you away. There is a tree blown down. Here are some young lambs: poor things! they are cold.

6. April is come, and the birds sing: the trees are in blossom, and the flowers are coming out. Now it rains: it rains: and the sun shines. There is a rainbow. O what fine colors! How beautiful is the rainbow! but it will not stay long; it is going away. It fades—it is quite gone—Farewell, rainbow.

7. May is very pleasant. Now Charles may walk out in the field. The air is sweet. The lambs are playing

about on the grass, among the sweet flowers. The trees are full of blossoms, and the birds sing. Pretty birds! sing for little Charles, he is a good boy. There is a robin-red-breast—Sing, robin.

8. June is come. Now it is very warm: we shall have roses, and all the sweet flowers of summer. You must get up early, and walk out to see the farmer mow the grass. Grass will make hay. How sweet the new hay smells! O it is very hot. Well, so much the better: you must make hay while the sun shines.

9. July is the hottest month. You must go under the trees, and play in the shade. Come, let us go in the garden. There is a bee upon the honey-suckle: he is getting honey: he will carry it to the hive, and save it for winter. Good bee! make honey for Charles.

10. August will bring us ripe apples, and pears, and water-melons, and green corn. Then September will come, and bring us good peaches. Hark! somebody has fired off a gun. They are shooting the poor birds. Here is a bird dropped just down at your feet. Poor thing! it is all bloody: how it flutters! it is going to die. Are you not sorry for the poor bird?

11. October is come, Charles, and the leaves are falling off the trees, and the flowers are almost gone: But here are some nuts, and a few grapes. Grapes make wine, and apples make cider, and nuts are good for boys to eat.

12. November brings rainy weather. No flowers, no hay-making now. Well, never mind it, we will sit by the fire, and read, and tell stories, and look at pictures. Where is Billy, and Harry, and Betsey? Now we will see who can spell best, and read best. Good children! you shall all have some cake.

13. December and Christmas are coming; and Betty

is very busy. What is she doing? She is paring apples, and chopping meat. What for, I wonder! O, to make mince pies. Do you like mince pies? Yes, they are very good; Christmas holidays, and mince pies, are very good for little boys.

14. In winter how white is the snow!
While boys on the ice are at play:
In spring the green herbage will grow,
With all the sweet blossoms of May.
What charms does the summer unfold!
While hay-makers breathe the sweet air,
And autumn brings treasures of gold;
The apple, the peach, and the pear.

On-ly, fish-es, floun-ces, kil-led, bel-lows, ti-ger spar-row, swal-low, twit-ters, pig-eon, tur-key, gob-bles, pea-cock, grass-hop-per, his-ses, gar-den, gra-vel, rol-ler, half-pen-ny, bar-row, gar-den-er, let-tuce, pars-ley, sa-lad, cur-rant, bush-es, ber-ry, la-dy, bee-tle, stock-ings, vic-tu-als, cold-er, win-dow, shiv-er, pul-led, sad-ly, beg-ging, cru-el, af-ter-wards. Him-self.

CHAPTER XXI. TWENTY-FIRST.

1. How many fingers have you got, little boy? Here are four fingers on this hand, and one thumb, that makes five. And five more on the other hand, makes ten. Ten fingers, and ten toes, I have got: and two legs. A horse has four legs, a goat has four legs, and puss has four legs; but a chicken has only two legs, a bird has only two legs, and Charles has only two legs.

2. How many legs have fishes? Fishes have no legs at all. They do not walk, they swim about in the water. Here is a fish that somebody has caught.

Poor little fish! see how it flounces about. It has a hook in its mouth. It will soon be dead. It cannot live out of the water, and Charles cannot live in the water.

3. Charles has got clothes to keep him warm. Feathers keep the birds warm, and wool makes the sheep warm. Can you climb a tree? Puss can climb a tree better than you. Ask puss to teach you. See how fast she climbs. Puss! do not catch the little birds on the trees; the birds must sing for Charles. O, naughty puss! she has caught a bird, and killed it.

4. The horse neighs. The cock crows. The ass brays. The bull bellows. The cow lows. The sheep bleats. The lion roars. The wolf howls. The tiger growls. The frog croaks. The sparrow chirps. The swallow twitters. The pigeon coos. The turkey gobbles. The peacock screams. The grasshopper chirps. The duck quacks. The owl hoots. The snake hisses. But little girls and boys talk.

5. Shall we go into the garden and see the flowers, and the apple-trees, and run about on the gravel-walk? Where is your roller? Come, roll the walk. If you work well, I will give you a half-penny a day. If you are a good boy, you shall have a little garden of your own, and a spade to dig with, and a hoe, and a rake, and a little wheel-barrow.

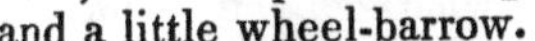

6. Do not let the weeds grow in your garden; pull them all up; weeds are good for nothing. You must

ask the gardener for some seeds, and you must sow them, and cover them with dirt. Here is some lettuce-seed, and some parsley-seed; sow them, and we shall have salad. Water your garden. Look at your currant-bushes, and the gooseberry-bushes; see how they grow.

7. Here is a lady-bird upon a leaf. It is red, and has black spots. Ah! it has got wings: it has flown away. There is a black beetle; catch it. How fast it runs! where is it gone? Into the ground: it makes a little hole, and runs into the ground.

8. It is cold, Charles, very cold. Pray what do they call it when it is cold? They call it winter. I wonder what poor little boys do, that have no fire to go to, and no shoes and stockings to keep them warm, and no good papa and mamma to take care of them, and give them victuals. Poor boys!

9. Do not cry, Charles, for here is a penny, and when you see one of those poor little boys, you shall give it him: he will go and buy a roll with it, for he is very hungry; and he will say, "Thank you, Charles, you are very good to me!"

10. I will tell you what, Charles; it will be a great deal colder, soon, and snow will come down; and when the poor robins fly against the window, you must open it and let them in. Well, what do you want, little robin? Only a few crumbs of bread. Give him some crumbs, and he will hop, hop, hop about the parlor, and sing for you. Do not let puss catch the robin.

11. There was a naughty boy, I do not know his name; but it was not Charles, nor George, nor Harry; for those are very pretty names: but there was a robin came in at his window one very cold morning—shiver—shiver, and its poor little body was almost frozen to death.

12. And he would not give the poor robin the least crumb of bread in the world, but pulled it about by the

tail, and hurt it sadly, so that it died. Now a little while after, the naughty boy's papa and mamma went away, and left him; and then he could not get victuals at all for himself: so he went about begging—Pray give me something to eat—I am very hungry.

13. And every body said, No, we shall give you none; for we do not love cruel naughty boys. You would not give the poor robin a few crumbs. So the naughty boy went about from one place to another, till at last he got into the woods, and was lost; for he did not know how to find his way anywhere: and then it grew dark: so he sat down, and cried sadly: and I believe the bears came and ate him up in the woods, for I never heard any thing about him afterwards.

Wi-ser, ta-ble, fly-ing, i-dle, rab-bit, mas-ter's, learn-ed, les-son, shi-ning, o-pen-ing, la-bors. Sa-tan, mis-chief, health-ful. Sup-pose, in-stead, im-prove, ac-count.

CHAPTER XXII. TWENTY-SECOND.

1. There was a little boy, he was not a big boy, for if he had been a big boy, I suppose he would have been wiser; but this was a little boy, not higher than the table; and his papa and mamma sent him to school: it was a very pleasant morning—the sun shone, and the birds sang in the trees. Now this little boy did not much love his book, for he was a silly little boy, as I told you; and he had a great mind to play, instead of going to school.

2. This silly boy saw a bee flying about, first on one flower, and then on another: so he said to the bee—Pretty bee! will you come and play with me? But the bee said, No, I must not be idle, I must go and gather honey. Then the little boy met a dog, and he

said, Dog! will you play with me? But the dog said No, I must not be idle, I am going to catch a rabbit for my master's dinner—I must make haste and catch it.

3. Then the little boy went by a hay-rick, and he saw a bird pulling some hay out of the hay-rick; and he said, Bird! will you come and play with me? But the bird said, No, I must not be idle, I must get some hay to build a nest with, and some moss, and some wool: so the bird flew away.

4. Then the little boy saw a horse: and he said, Horse! will you play with me? But the horse said, No, I must not be idle, I must go and plow, or else there will be no corn to make bread of.

5. Then the little boy thought with himself, What! is nobody idle? then little boys must not be idle neither. So he made haste, and went to school, and learned his lesson very well; and the master said he was a very good boy.

6 How doth the little busy bee
  Improve each shining hour,
And gather honey all the day,
  From every opening flower!

With how much art she builds her cell!
  How neat she spreads the wax!
And labors hard to store it well,
  With the sweet food she makes.

7 In works of labor and of skill,
  I would be busy too;
For Satan finds some mischief still,
  For idle hands to do.
In books, or works, or healthful play,
  Let my first years be past;
That I may give for every day,
  Some good account at last.

Quar-rel, na-tur-ed, fel-low, lov-ing, clev-er-ly, let-ters, al-pha-bet, vow-els, syl-la-ble, con-so-nants, com-ma, co-lon, pe-ri-od, nine-ty, Ger-man-town, Bos-ton, hun-dred, thou-sand, Lon-don, heart-ed, gath-er-ing, Sav-ior's, un-cle, To-by, buz-zing, gold-smith, ti-ed, cram-med, pock-et, gi-ant, pas-ture, clo-ver, but-ter-fly, whith-er, go-est, sim-ple-ton, watch-es, help-less, near-er, speck-led, dif-fer-ent, mo-ment, o-blig-ing, o-be-di-ent, di-rect-ly, un-til, at-tend, de-vour, ex-am-ine, en joy-ing, re-gale, thy-self. Sem-i-co-lon, Phil-a-del-phi-a, ad-mi-ra-tion, in-ter-ro-ga-tion.

CHAPTER XXIII. TWENTY-THIRD.

1. Billy was a very good boy; he would always do as he was bid; he would go quick and come quick, and shut the door after him. He would never quarrel and do mischief, but was always good-natured and obliging to his play-fellows, and every-body loved him.

2. Billy was always obedient to his parents, and lov-ing to his brothers and sisters: when he was in school,

he would sit still, and mind his book; and when school was out, he would go directly home, and not play by the way, as bad boys do.

3. Billy loved his book and his school, and would play with none but good boys. He said if he played with bad boys, he was afraid he would learn to be bad too; and he said very right, for good boys should never play with bad boys.

4. Billy is only five years old, and he can spell all the hard words in his lesson; and begins to read cleverly. He does not go to play until he has got his lesson: he minds the wise saying, Business first, and then pleasure: he says, that good boys get their lesson first, and then play.

5. Billy knows that a cow will give more milk than a goat: he knows that milk is good to eat; and that butter and cheese are made of milk; and that whey is made of milk. He says that cows are very good to give milk for little boys.

6. Billy knows that there are twenty-six letters in the alphabet; and that six of them are vowels. He says there can be no syllable without a vowel; a, e, i, o, u, y, are vowels, and all the other letters are

consonants. He says, if you would be wise, you must attend to your vowels and consonants.—Let this be your plan—Learn all that you can.

7. Billy knows, when a boy reads, he should always mind his stops. He knows the comma , semicolon ; colon : period . interrogation ? and admiration ! He says, you must stop at a , while you can say one—at a ; while you can say, one, two—at a : one, two, three—at a . one, two, three, four; and at the ? and ! you must stop nearly as long as at the period.

8. Billy knows that some places are a great way off. He knows that it is ninety-six miles from Philadelphia to New-York, when it is only six to Germantown. He knows that Boston is three hundred miles from Philadelphia; and somebody told him that it was more than three thousand miles to London.

9. Billy was always tender-hearted, as all good boys are; he could never like to see naughty boys kill bees when they were gathering honey from the flowers. He would never catch flies and pull off their wings, and stick pins through them, as bad boys do. He said that God made the flies to fly about, and it is very cruel to stick pins through them. How they whip the poor horses when they haul wood!

10. Billy says that our Savior's golden rule is, to DO TO OTHERS AS WE WOULD HAVE OTHERS DO TO US, and this is certainly the best rule in the world; for if we are kind and good to others, God will certainly be kind and good to us.

Teach me to feel another's woe,
To hide the faults I see;
That mercy I to others show,
That mercy show to me.

11. Billy said that uncle Toby did to others as he would have others do to him. Once as he was eating

dinner, a fly came buzzing about his face, and he caught it. Now I have thee, thou little rogue, says uncle Toby; but I will not kill thee: No, I will not hurt thee. So he took the fly to the door, and said to it, Go, poor rogue, I will not hurt a hair of thy head: go, fly away; the world is wide enough for us both.

12. Billy says that once a naughty boy caught a little goldsmith; he tied it fast with a thread, and would not let it go: then he pulled off one of its legs, and crammed it into his dirty pocket, and hurt the poor thing very much.—Naughty boy! how would you like to have a great giant catch you, and pull off one of your arms, and break your bones, and then cram you into his pocket? You would not like it at all: so the goldsmith does not like it.

13. Once Billy found a grasshopper in the room, and the maid was going to kill it: but Billy said, she must not kill it, she must give it to him. So he took it to the door, just as uncle Toby did the fly, and said to it, Go, little grasshopper, hop away; I will not kill thee; No, I will not hurt thee: the world is wide enough for us both: go, little grasshopper, hop away to the pasture, and eat white clover.

14. Now I will tell you what Billy said to the butterfly:—Butterfly! whither goest thou, little simpleton? Seest thou not that hungry bird watching thee? His bill is sharp, and ready open to devour thee: come, then, come hither; he will be afraid of me, and will not then dare to touch thee.—Butterfly! pretty butterfly! come and rest on this flower that I hold in my hand.

15. Butterfly! I will not pull off thy wings, nor hurt thee: No, no; thou art little and helpless, like my little sister. I only wish to look on thee nearer; I want to see thy little head, and to examine thy long body, and thy beautiful wings, speckled with a thousand different

colors.—Buttterfly! pretty butterfly! come and rest on this flower that I hold in my hand.

16. Butterfly, I will not keep thee long; I know thou hast not long to live. When the summer is over, thou wilt be no more: and as for me, I shall be only six years old. Thou hast not a moment to lose from enjoying this short life: but thou mayest feed and regale thyself all the time I look at thee.—Butterfly! pretty butterfly! come, rest on this flower that I hold in my hand.

Pray-ers, pi-ty, rag-ged, A-gur's, chap-ter, Pro-verbs, va-ni-ty, rich-es, wash-ed, satch-el, Ches-ter, Lan-cas-ter, Bur-ling-ton, Je-sus, suf-fer, king-dom, bles-sed, run-ning, ge-ne-ral, Wash-ing-ton, con-stant-ly, ser-vi-tude, in-fant, glo-ri-ous, em-pires, scep-tres, par-son, law-yer, pre-si-dent, ei-ther, fin-est, or-a-tor, kis-sed, tur-tle, ba-lan-ced, cen-tre.

CHAPTER XX. TWENTIETH.

MORE ABOUT BILLY.

1. When Billy went to bed he always said his prayers, and desired that God would bless his papa and mamma, and his brothers and sisters: he prayed that God would have pity on poor little boys and girls who are hungry, and cold, and ragged, and have no friends to take care of them.

2. Billy found Agur's prayer in the xxxth chapter of Proverbs: and here it is:—Two things have I desired of thee; deny me them not before I die. Remove far from me vanity and lies; give me neither poverty nor riches; feed me with food convenient for me, lest I be full, and deny thee, and say, Who is the Lord? Or lest I be poor, and steal, and take the name of God in vain.

3. When Billy got up in the morning, he washed his hands and face clean, and said his prayers; then flew away to his satchel for his book; and while the maid was getting breakfast for him to eat, he was getting some good lesson to read. He could spell Chester, Lancaster, and Burlington.

4. Then were brought unto Christ little children, that he should put his hands on them, and pray: and the disciples rebuked them: but Jesus said, Suffer little children to come unto me, and forbid them not; for of such is the kingdom of heaven. And he laid his hands on them, and blessed them.

5. Once Billy came running to his mamma; he was almost out of breath; he said that General Washington was coming to town, and they were going to fire the great guns. Hark! says he, do you hear the drums?—Then his mamma said to him, Come, Billy, can you say a speech for these ladies?—Billy would always do as he was bid—he made his bow, and began:

6. Americans! place constantly before your eyes the deplorable scene of your servitude, and the enchanting picture of your deliverance. Begin with the infant in his cradle: let the first word he lisps be WASHINGTON!

O Washington! thrice-glorious name!
What due rewards can man decree;
Empires are far below thy aim,
And sceptres have no charms for thee;
Virtue alone has thy regard,
And she shall be thy great reward.

7. The ladies were all delighted to hear Billy speak so well. One said he should be a parson; another said he should be a lawyer; and another said he should be the president of the United States: but Billy said he could not be either, unless his mamma gave him leave. Then the finest lady of them all said to him, Come here, my sweet little orator. So she kissed him, and gave him two great red apples.—Now you may go and see General Washington.

8. Harry—says Billy, who made the world? I do not know, says Harry. Well, then, says Billy, I will tell you: God made the world, and all things that are in it. He made the sun, and the moon, and the stars; and all the birds that fly in the air. God made the water, and all the fishes that are in the rivers.

9. Harry—says Billy, what do you think the world stands on? I do not know, says Harry; but I will tell you what our old Tom says.—Our old Tom says that the world stands on a great turtle: but he cannot tell what the turtle stands on. Well, says Billy, I will tell you what my papa says.—My papa says that the world does not stand on any thing; but, it is balanced on its own centre, and goes round the sun, in open space, once every year.

10. Once every year, is my birth-day, says Billy. Ah, now I remember, this very day is my birth-day: I am glad my sister told me of it; for if she had not, I should not have thought of it. Well, I wonder what my papa will give me! I hope he will give me some pretty book that has pictures in it: and I hope my mamma will give me a pencil, and then I will try to draw a little bird.

11. Great God, to thee my voice I raise,
To thee my youngest hours belong;
I would begin my life with praise,
Till growing years improve the song.
'Tis to thy sovereign grace I owe,
That I was born on Christian ground,
Where streams of heavenly mercy flow,
And words of sweet salvation sound.
I would not change my native land
For rich Peru, with all her gold;
A nobler prize is in my hand,
Than East or Western Indies hold.
Thy glorious promises, O Lord!
Kindle my hopes and my desires:
While all the preachers of thy word,
Warn me to 'scape eternal fires.
Thy praise shall still employ my breath,
Since thou hast mark'd my way to heaven:
Nor will I run the road to death,
And waste the blessings thou hast given.

Coun-sel, shin-eth, bright-er, per-fect, tow-ards, wor-ship, mer-cy, hon-or, her-it-age, trou-ble, en-e-mies. En-tice, re-frain, de-light-eth, o-bey, en-dur-eth, cre-a-ted, for-ev-er, de-liv-er-ance. Re-deem-er, at-tend.

CHAPTER XXV. TWENTY-FIFTH.

GOOD ADVICE FOR CHILDREN.

1. My son, hear the counsel of thy father, and forsake not the law of thy mother. If sinners entice thee to sin, consent thou not: walk not in the way with them; refrain thy feet from their path, for their feet run to evil, and make haste to shed blood.

2. Be a good child; mind your book; love your school, and strive to learn. Tell no tales; call no ill names; play not with bad boys; use no ill words at play; spend your time well; live in peace, and shun all strife. This is the way to make good men love you; and to save your soul from pain and woe.

3. Put thy trust in God, and he will keep thee from all harm. Let not God go out of thy mind, for He is thy guard and thy guide. God knows what is best for thee; to Him thou must look for help.

4. God does mind all that we say and do. He sees us when we go out, and when we come in. If we pray to God with a pure mind, he will hear us, and help us.

We must love those who do not love us, and pray for those who hate us.

5. My son, you must love God with all your heart, and with all your soul: He made you, He gives you life, and is very kind to all those who put their trust in him. O praise the Lord, all ye sons of men, for his mercy endureth for ever.

6. Seek the Lord in thy youth, and serve him with all thy heart, soul, and might. He is near to us at all times, and he knows all our thoughts. He shows us what is right, and what is wrong; and he calls to us thus:—My son! give me thine heart.

7. Trust in the Lord, and he will guide thee in the way of good men. The path of the just is a light that shineth brighter and brighter unto the perfect day. We must do all the good we can, to all men; for this is well pleasing in the sight of God who made us. He delighteth to see his children walk in love, and do good one to another.

8. My duty towards God is, to believe in him, to fear him, and to love him with all my heart, with all my mind, with all my soul, and with all my strength: to worship him, to give him thanks, to put my whole trust in him, to call upon him, to honor his holy name, and his word, and to serve him truly all the days of my life.

9. There is but one God, the maker of all things, both in heaven and in earth. He is holy, just, and good. He fills heaven and earth with his wisdom, mercy, and truth. He will love those who love him; and he will bless all good children who love, honor, and obey their parents.

10. O give thanks unto the Lord, for he is good; for his mercy endureth for ever.

O give thanks unto the Lord, who created the heavens, and the earth, and the seas; for his mercy endureth for ever.

O give thanks unto the Lord, who maketh the sun to rule the day, and the moon and stars to rule the night, for his mercy endureth for ever.

11. From all who dwell below the skies,
Let the Creator's praise arise;
Let the Redeemer's name be sung,
Through every land, by every tongue.
Eternal are thy mercies, Lord,
Eternal truth attends thy word:
Thy praise shall sound from shore to shore,
Till suns shall rise and set no more.

CHAPTER XXVI. TWENTY-SIXTH.

WORDS WHIGH ARE ALIKE IN SOUND, BUT DIFFERENT IN SPELLING AND SIGNIFICATION.

A

Ac-ci-dence, a grammar
Ac-ci-dents, things happening by chance
Ail, to be sick
Ale, a kind of beer
Air, the fluid we breathe
Heir, one who inherits an estate
All, the whole
Awl, a tool for piercing
Al-tar, a place for sacrifice
Al-ter, to change
An-ker, a measure of brandy
An-chor, a heavy iron to hold a ship
Ant, an insect
Aunt, an uncle's wife
As-sent, agreement
As-cent, the act of rising
Ate, did eat
Eight, a number
Au-ger, a tool to bore with
Au-gur, a fortune-teller
Aught, anything
Ought, in duty bound
As-sist-ance, help, aid
As-sist-ants, those who afford aid
At-tend-ance, presence, waiting
At-tend-ants, waiters, servants

B

Bail, surety, security
Bale, a package of goods
Bait, a temptation
Bate, to reduce, to take less
Baize, a coarse cloth
Bays, wreaths

Bald, without hair on the head
Bawl-ed, cried out
Ball, a round substance
Bawl, to cry aloud
Bar-ba-ry, a place in Africa
Bar-ber-ry, a small red fruit
Bear, to suffer anything
Bare, naked
Base, mean, vile
Bass, a part in music
Be, to exist
Bee, an insect
Beach, a shore of the sea
Beech, a kind of tree
Beat, to strike
Beet, a garden root
Beer, malt liquor
Bier, a carriage for the dead
Bell, a sounding instrument
Belle, a handsome lady
Ber-ry, a small fruit
Bu-ry, to put under ground
Blew, did blow
Blue, one of the seven colors
Board, a thin plank
Bor-ed, did bore
Boar, a small swine
Bore, to make a hole
Bolt, a fastening
Boult, to sift grain
Bold, daring
Bowl-ed, did bowl
Bow, to bend
Bough, a branch of a tree
Bow, a weapon for shooting
Beau, a fine gentleman
Braid, to plait anything
Bray-ed, did bray
Brake, a bramble
Break, to open by force
Bread, ground and baked wheat, &c.
Bred, brought up
Breast, a part of the body
Brest, a city of France
Brews, maketh beer
Bruise, to hurt
By, near
Buy, to purchase
But, except
Butt, a large cask

C

Cain, Abel's brother
Cane, a staff to walk with
Ca-len-dar, an almanac
Ca-len-der, to smooth cloth
Call, to cry out
Caul, a part of the bowels
Can-non, a great gun
Ca-non, a rule, a law
Cause, a reason
Caws, the cry of a crow
Ceil, to cover a roof
Seal, to fasten a letter, &c.
Ceil-ing, the top of a roof
Seal-ing, setting a seal
Cell, a hut
Sell, to exchange for money
Cel-lar, a vault
Sel-ler, one who exchanges values
Cense, a public tax
Sense, understanding
Cere, to cover with wax
Sear, to burn
Seer, a prophet
Cent, a copper coin of the United States
Scent, smell, odor
Sent, transmitted

Ces-sion, a giving up
Ses-sion, a sitting of a court
Cha-grin, to vex, to mortify
Sha-green, a fish's skin
Chaste, pure, virtuous
Cha-sed, did pursue
Chol-er, rage, anger
Col-lar, a band for the neck
Coun-sel, advice
Coun-cil, an assembly
Chron-i-cal, relating to time
Chron-i-cle, a history
Cinque, the number *five*, in French
Sink, to go down, a drain
Ci-on, a sprout
Zi-on, a mountain in the East
Cite, to summon, to quote
Site, a situation
Sight, vision, a view
Clause, a sentence
Claws, the feet of a beast
Climb, to ascend, to go up
Clime, a region, a country
Close, to shut up
Clothes, wearing apparel
Coarse, large, not fine
Course, a career, order of succession
Cof-fer, a chest for money
Cough-er, one who coughs
Com-ple-ment, the full number
Com-pli-ment, flattery
Cor-res-pond-ence, intercourse by letter
Cor-res-pond-ents, those who have intercourse
Cous-in, an uncle's child
Coz-en, to cheat
Crews, persons in charge of ships
Cruise, to sail in pursuit of gain
Crew-el, twisted yarn
Cru-el, unfeeling, inhuman
Cur-rant, a kind of fruit
Cur-rent, a running stream
Cyg-net, a young swan
Sig-net, a seal

D

Dam, to stop or collect water
Damn, to condemn
Dane, a native of Denmark
Deign, to grant
Day, twenty-four hours
Dey, the governor of Algiers
Dear, costly, beloved
Deer, a wild animal
De-pend-ence, reliance
De-pend-ants, those who rely upon others
De-sert, to forsake, to leave
Des-sert, the last course of a meal
Dire, dreadful, sad
Dy-er, a colorer of cloth
Doe, a female deer
Dough, bread prepared for baking
Dol-lar, a silver and gold coin of the United States
Dol-or, grief, sorrow
Dun, a brown color
Done, finished

E

Ere, before
E'er, contraction of ever

F

Fain, gladly, willingly
Fane, a temple
Feign, to dissemble, to pretend
Faint, languid, dim
Feint, a pretence
Fair, beautiful, clear
Fare, food, passage money
Feat, an action, an exploit
Feet, parts of the body, the lower extremities
Fir, a sort of pine tree
Fur, the hair of animals
Flea, an insect
Flee, to run from danger
Flew, did fly
Flue, a passage, soft down
Flour, ground wheat
Flower, a blossom
Forth, abroad
Fourth, next in order to third
Fore, in front
Four, three and one added
Foul, unclean, filthy
Fowl, a winged animal
Frays, quarrels, fights
Phrase, a mode of speech
Freeze, to congeal with cold
Frieze, a coarse kind of cloth

G

Gait, manner of walking
Gate, an entrance
Gall, a bitter substance
Gaul, a native of France
Gild, to adorn with gold
Guild, a corporation
Gilt, covered with gold
Guilt, criminality, sin
Glaire, the white of an egg
Glare, to shine brightly, to dazzle
Go-er, one who proceeds
Gore, clotted blood
Grate, fire-place for coals
Great, of large size
Great-er, larger, of more bulk
Grat-er, a rough instrument
Grease, soft fat
Greece, a country in the south of Europe
Greaves, armor for the legs
Grieves, regrets, laments
Groan, a deep sigh of pain
Grown, increased, enlarged
Guest, a visiter
Guess-ed, did guess or surmise

H

Hail, a word of salutation, frozen rain
Hale, sound, healthy
Hair, covering of the head
Hare, a swift running animal
Hall, a large high room
Haul, to drag along
Hart, the male deer
Heart, the seat of life
Heal, to cure a wound
Heel, the hinder part of the foot
He'll, contraction of he will
Hear, to perceive sounds
Here, present, not absent
Heard, listened to
Herd, a drove of animals
Height, elevation
Hight, called or named

Hue, color, tint
Hew, to cut with an ax
Hugh, a man's name
Hie, to hasten
High, lofty, elevated
High-er, more elevated
Hire, wages, salary
Him, the person spoken of
Hymn, a song to God
Ho, an exclamation
Hoe, a garden tool

I

I, the person speaking, myself
Eye, the organ of sight
In, gone from without
Inn, a tavern, a hotel
In-no-cence, harmlessness
In-no-cents, young babes
In-tense, powerful, vehement
In-tents, purposes, plans

J

Jew-ry, a name for Judea
Ju-ry, twelve men to decide causes in courts

K

Kill, to destroy life
Kiln, a place for burning bricks, &c.

L

Lacks, wants, needs
Lax, loose, careless
Lade, to dip water, to fill ships with freight
Laid, placed, deposited
Lain, did lie
Lane, a narrow street
Leaf, the green part of a tree
Lief, willingly, readily
Led, directed, guided
Lead, a soft, heavy metal
Leek, a kind of onion
Leak, to run out of a small opening
Les-sen, to make less, to diminish
Les-son, a task, a division of a book
Let-tice, a woman's name
Let-tuce, a salad, herb
Lev-ee, audience at court
Lev-y, to lay taxes, to seize
Li-ar, one who avoids or perverts the truth
Li-er, one who reclines
Lyre, a musical instrument
Lick-er-ish, over-nice
Lic-or-ice, a sweet root
Limb, a part of a body or tree
Limn, to paint, to depict
Lo, behold
Low, humble, mean, the reverse of high
Lone, single, without company
Loan, money, &c., lent
Lore, learning, knowledge
Low-er, more low

M

Made, did form or produce
Maid, an unmarried woman
Mail, a bag of letters, a shirt of steel rings
Male, one of the two sexes
Main, the ocean, chief
Mane, the hair on a horse's neck
Maize, Indian corn
Maze, an intricate place

Mall, a wooden hammer
Maul, to beat, to strike
Man-ner, style, custom, form
Man-or, jurisdiction over land
Mare, the female horse
May-or, chief magistrate of a city
Mar-shal, an officer
Mar-tial, warlike
Mar-ten, a kind of swallow
Mar-tin, a man's name
Mead, honey and water fermented, a grassy meadow
Mede, a native of Media
Meed, a reward
Mean, low, niggardly
Mein, look, appearance
Meat, flesh of animals
Meet, to come together
Mete, fit, measure
Med-al, a coin given as a reward
Med-dle, to interfere
Med-lar, a kind of apple
Med-dler, a busybody
Mes-sage, a verbal errand
Mes-suage, a house and adjoining grounds
Met-al, a hard compact body
Met-tle, courage, spirit
Mewl, to cry as a child
Mule, a beast of burden
Mews, the cries of a cat, stables
Muse, to ponder, to reflect
Might, power, strength
Mite, a small insect found in cheese
Mi-ner, a worker in a mine
Mi-nor, aged less than 21
Moan, to lament in a low tone
Mown, cut with a scythe
Moat, a ditch for water
Mote, a particle of dust
More, a greater quantity
Mow-er, one who cuts grass or grain

N

Nat, an abbreviation of Nathaniel
Gnat, a small stinging fly
Nap, a short sleep
Knap, to snap, to bite
Na-val, relating to ships
Na-vel, a part of the body
Naught, bad, worthless
Nought, nothing, the figure 0
Nay, not only so
Neigh, the voice of a horse
Nave, the middle of a wheel
Knave, a rascal, a scoundrel
Need, want, necessity
Knead, to work dough
Neal, to temper by heat
Kneel, to bend on the knee
Nell, abbreviation of Eleanor
Knell, the sound of a tolling bell
New, fresh, modern
Knew, did know
Night, the darkness following sunset
Knight, a military rank
Nit, the egg of a louse
Knit, to weave without a loom
No, a word of denial, not so
Know, to be informed
None, not any, no one
Nun, a female recluse

Nose, the organ of smell
Knows, understands, apprehends

O

Oar, an instrument for rowing
O'er, contraction of over
Ore, metal unrefined
Our, belonging to us
Hour, twenty-fourth part of a day

P

Pail, a wooden bucket
Pale, wan, white
Pain, torment, distress
Pane, a square of glass
Pair, a couple, two
Pare, to cut off thinly
Pear, a kind of fruit
Pall, the covering to a coffin
Paul, one of Christ's apostles
Pan-el, a part of the frame of a door
Pan-nel, a kind of saddle
Pa-tience, endurance
Pa-tients, sick persons
Pause, a stop
Paws, the feet of a quadruped
Peace, quietness, freedom from war
Piece, a part, a measure of cloth
Peak, a point, the top
Pique, an affront
Peal, a succession of sounds
Peel, a rind or skin
Pe-ter, one of the 12 apostles
Pe-tre, nitre, a chemical substance
Place, situation, position
Plaice, a species of fish
Plain, clear, evident
Plane, a joiner's tool, a flat surface
Plait, a fold
Plate, wrought silver or gold, a vessel to eat from
Pleas, apologies, excuses
Please, to delight, to gratify
Plum, a kind of fruit
Plumb, a leaden weight
Pole, a long stick or mast
Poll, a name for the head
Pore, a passage through the skin, to look intently
Pour, to flow rapidly
Prac-tice, use, habit
Prac-tise, to exercise
Praise, commendation, approval
Prays, entreateth, desireth
Pray, to beseech, to petition
Prey, plunder, booty
Pres-ence, state of being present
Pres-ents, gifts, gratuities
Pri-er, an inquisitive person
Pri-or, former, previous, the head of a convent
Pries, searches into
Prize, to value, to esteem
Prin-ci-pal, head, chief
Prin-ci-ple, a first cause
Prof-it, gain, advantage
Proph-et, a foreteller

Q

Quean, a worthless woman
Queen, the wife of a king

Quire, 24 sheets of paper
Choir, a set of singers

R

Rain, water from the clouds
Rein, part of a bridle
Reign, to rule
Raise, to set up, to elevate
Rays, beams of light
Raze, to demolish, to ruin
Rase, to blot out
Rap, to strike smartly
Wrap, to fold together
Ra-zor, a tool used in removing beard
Rais-er, one who raises
Red, one of the seven colors
Read, perused, studied
Reek, smoke, vapor
Wreak, to revenge
Rest, repose, quiet
Wrest, to force
Retch, to vomit
Wretch, a miserable person
Rime, a white frost
Rhyme, to agree in sound
Rice, a sort of grain
Rise, origin, beginning
Rig-ger, one who accoutres
Rig-or, severity, hardness
Right, just, true
Rite, a ceremony
Write, to form letters
Wright, a workman
Road, the highway
Rode, did ride
Row-ed, propelled by oars
Roe, a female deer
Row, a rank, to move with an oar
Rote, memory
Wrote, did write
Ruff, a neckcloth
Rough, uneven
Rung, did ring or sound
Wrung, twisted
Rye, a sort of grain
Wry, crooked

S

Sail, canvass of a ship
Sale, the act of selling
Sa-tire, keen language
Sa-tyr, a god of the woods
Scene, part of a play, a view
Seen, beheld
Seine, a fish net
Scil-ly, an island's name
Sil-ly, foolish, weak
Sea, a part of the ocean
See, to behold, to observe
Seam, to join by sewing
Seem, to appear to be
Sear, to burn, to dry up
Seer, a prophet
Seas, great waters
Sees, observes, notices
Seize, to lay hold of
Seign-ior, the ruler of the Turks
Sen-ior, elder
Shear, to cut with shears
Shire, a county
Shoar, a prop
Shore, the bank of a river
Shone, did shine or glisten
Shown, made to appear
Sire, a father, a king
Sigh-er, one who laments

Sine, a term in geometry
Sign, a token, an evidence
Slight, neglect
Sleight, dexterity
Sloe, a wild plum
Slow, dull, tardy
Soar, to mount upward
Sore, diseased
Sow-er, one who scatters seed
So, thus, in this manner
Sow, to scatter seed
Sew, to work with a needle
Sole, the bottom of the foot
Soul, the spirit of a man
Stair, a step
Stare, to look earnestly
Steal, to take without liberty
Steel, hardened iron
Stile, a step in a field
Style, manner of expression
Straight, direct, undeviating
Strait, a narrow passage
Suc-cor, help, aid
Suck-er, a young shoot
Sew-er, a drain under ground
Su-er, one who begs or entreats
Sum, the total of anything
Some, a part, a portion
Sun, the light of day
Son, a male child
Sut-tle, net weight
Sub-tle, cunning, artful

T

Tacks, small nails
Tax, a rate, an impost
Tail, the lower part
Tale, a story, a recital
Tare, weight allowed by custom
Tear, to rend, to pull asunder
Team, a pair of horses or oxen
Teem, to give birth to, to abound
Tear, water from the eye
Tier, a rank or row of anything
Their, belonging to them
There, in that place
The, an article in grammar
Thee, the person addressed
Throne, a monarch's seat of state
Thrown, cast, hurled
Tide, ebb and flow of the sea
Tied, fastened, bound
Time, the measure of duration or existence
Thyme, a kind of herb
Told, related, described
Toll-ed, did ring
To, unto
Too, likewise
Two, a couple, twice one
Toe, a part of the foot
Tow, to drag along
Threw, did throw
Through, from end to end

V

Vale, a space between two hills
Veil, a covering for the face
Vain, proud, foolish
Vein, a blood-vessel, or passage
Vain, useless, needless
Vane, a weather-guide

Vi-al, a small bottle
Vi-ol, a musical instrument

W

Wade, to walk through water
Weigh-ed, balanced in a scale
Wait, to tarry, to linger
Weight, heaviness, gravity
Wail, to lament
Wale, the mark of a whip
Waist, the middle of the body
Waste, to destroy, to spend lavishly
Wall, the side of a house
Waul, to cry like a cat
Ware, merchandise, an article of sale
Wear, to waste away
Way, a road or passage
Weigh, to poise, to balance
Weak, feeble, powerless
Week, seven days
Wean, to put from the breast
Ween, to imagine, to think
Wether, a kind of sheep
Weather, state of the air
Wood, timber, the trunk and branches of a tree
Would, was willing

Y

Yew, a churchyard tree
You, the person addressed
Ewe, a female sheep

CHAPTER XXVII. TWENTY-SEVENTH.

WORDS WHICH ARE SOMEWHAT SIMILAR IN SOUND, AND WHICH ARE VULGARLY SOUNDED ALIKE, BUT WHICH SHOULD BE PRONOUNCED DISTINCTLY DIFFERENTLY.

A

A-BEL, a man's name
A-ble, having power
Ac-cept, to receive
Ex-cept, to leave out, to reject
Ac-cess, an approach
Ex-cess, a superfluity
A-chor, the name of a valley
A-cre, 4840 square yards
Acts, deeds, doings
Ax, an instrument to cut with
Ask, to request, to solicit
Af-fect, to move, to soften
Ef-fect, to bring to pass
Al-low-ed, granted, permitted
A-loud, with a noise
Ar-rant, notorious
Er-rand, a message
Er-rant, wandering

B

Bacon, smoked hog's flesh
Bea-con, a guide, a lighthouse
Bal-lot, a paper used in voting
Bal-lad, a simple song
Bal-let, a dance
Bar-on, a title of honor, a rank
Bar-ren, unfruitful
Bile, an inflamed swelling
Boil, to bustle, to agitate

Borne, supported
Bourne, a boundary line
Born, brought forth
Boar, a male swine
Bore, a tiresome fellow
Boor, an uneducated person
Boy, a male child or lad
Buoy, to bear up
Breach, a broken place
Breech, part of a gun
Breach-es, broken places
Breech-es, a part of a man's dress
Bri-dal, a wedding
Bri-dle, reins for a horse
Brit-ain, a name for England
Brit-on, a native of England
Bre-ton, a place in France
Bust, an image of half the body
Burst, to break or fly open

C

Can-did, honest, free, open
Can-di-ed, thickened, hardened
Cap-i-tal, money invested
Cap-i-tol, a public building
Cap-tor, one who takes a prize
Cap-ture, to take captive
Car-at, a weight of 4 grains
Car-rot, a garden root
Ca-ret, a mark of omission in writing
Cents, plural of cent
Since, afterward
Cen-sure, to blame
Cen-ser, a pan for incense
Cen-tu-ry, one hundred years
Cen-tau-ry, a kind of plant
Sen-try, a guard
Chews, grinds with the teeth
Choose, to select
Ci-vil, kind, complaisant
Sev-ille, a city in Spain
Cit, an inhabitant of a city
Sit, to be seated
Set, to put, to fix
Coat, an article of dress
Cote, a sheepfold, a cottage
Quote, to cite an author's words
Cof-fin, a case for the dead
Cough-ing, relieving the lungs
Con-fi-dant, a trusty friend
Con-fi-dent, positive
Con-cert, a harmony of sounds
Con-sort, a wife
Cork, to close a bottle
Calk, to stop leaks in a ship
Coun-cil, an assembly
Coun-sel, advice, instruction
Creak, to make a harsh noise
Creek, a bay
Crick, a pain in the neck, &c.
Cym-bal, a musical instrument
Sym-bol, a sign, a representation
Cy-press, a funeral tree
Cy-prus, an island in the Mediterranean

D

De-scent, a going down
Dis-sent, disagreement
Dew, moisture, dampness
Due, a debt
Do, to act, to person

Dis-ease, sickness
Dis-seize, to dispossess
De-cease, to die
Dome, an arched roof
Doom, a sentence, fate
Doze, to slumber gently
Does, the state of doing
Dust, fine particles of dirt
Durst, dared

E

Eat-en, devoured
Ea-ton, a man's name
En-vy, to grudge
En-voy, an embassador
Ex-er-cise, to use, to labor
Ex-or-cise, to cast out spirits
Ex-tant, now in being
Ex-tent, utmost limits

F

Fel-low, a companion
Fel-loe, the rim of a wheel
Fel-ler, one who hews down
File, to smooth metals
Foil, to defeat, to overcome
Fool, an idiot
Full, complete measure
Francis, the name of a man
Frances, the name of a wo-

G

Ges-ture, a movement of the body
Jest-er, one who makes sport
Grand-er, more grand
Gran-deur, splendor
Groat, an old coin worth four pence sterling
Grot, a cavern for coolness

H

Harsh, rough, severe
Hash, minced meat
Heav-en, the habitation of God
Ha-ven, a harbor, a shelter
Hole, a hollow place
Whole, perfect, entire
Ho-ly, sacred, religious
Whol-ly, fully, entirely
Hoop, a circular band
Whoop, an Indian war cry

I

I-dle, unemployed, lazy
I-dol, an image of a god
I'll, contraction of I will
Oil, liquid fat
Im-pos-tor, a pretender, a cheat
Im-pos-ture, fraud, deception
In-ge-ni-ous, skilful, inventive
In-gen-u-ous, candid, frank

J

Jest, a joke, a witty speech
Just, right, honest

K

Ken-nel, a hut for dogs
Ker-nel, the seed of a fruit
Kine, a name for cows
Coin, money made of metal
Kind, benevolent, feeling
Coin-ed, did coin

L

Le-gis-la-tor, a law-maker
Le-gis-la-ture, an assembly which makes laws
Lieu, room, stead
Loo, a game at cards

Line, a string
Loin, the lower part of the back
Load, a burden of freight
Low-ed, did low or bellow

M

Marsh, wet, low ground
Mash, to beat into a mass
Mesh, a space in a net
Mild, pleasant, gentle
Mile, 1760 yards
Mind, the reasoning power
Mine, belonging to me
Mus-lin, cloth made of cotton
Muz-zling, tying or closing the mouth
Mole, a small blind animal
Mould, to shape, to form

N

News, a fresh account of events
Noose, a slipping knot

O

Of, belonging to it
Off, distant from
Oh, an exclamation of pain
Owe, to be indebted
Or-der, method, system
Or-dure, dung, filth

P

Pal-ace, the house of a king or noble
Pal-las, a goddess of the ancients
Pal-ate, the organ of taste
Pal-ette, a painter's tablet
Pal-let, a small bed
Pas-tor, a clergyman
Pas-ture, land for grazing
Pa-tron, one who aids or assists
Pat-tern, a specimen, a copy
Pies, a crust baked with fruit, &c. in it
Poise, to balance, to weigh
Pi-late, a Roman name
Pi-lot, the guide of a vessel
Pil-lar, a column, a support
Pil-low, a bag of feathers for a bed
Pint, a measure of four gills
Point, a sharp end, a stop
Poach, to boil or heat slightly
Porch, an entrance, a door
Pop-lar, a kind of tree
Pop-u-lar, much liked
Pop-u-lace, the people of a city
Pop-u-lous, full of people
Pre-ce-dent, an example
Pres-i-dent, one who governs
Press-er, one who works at a press
Pres-sure, weight over or against
Prin-ces, the sons of kings
Prin-cess, the daughter of a king

Q

Qua-ver, a vibration in music
Quiv-er, a case for arrows

R

Rack, to torture
Wreck, a ruined ship
Rai-sin, a dried grape
Rea-son, a cause
Red-dish, of a red color
Rad-ish, a garden-root

Rel-ic, a remnant
Rel-ict, a widow
Rood, one fourth of an acre
Rude, rough, uncivil
Re-al, a Spanish coin
Roy-al, kingly, noble

S

Sab-bath, first day of the week
Sa-ba-oth, armies, hosts
Sal-a-ry, stated wages
Cel-e-ry, a salad herb
Sa-ver, one who protects
Sa-vor, odor, smell
Sav-ior, a name of Christ
Sects, parties in religion
Sex, a distinction in animals
Sward, a grassy turf
Sword, a weapon used in war
Soar-ed, did rise in the air
Soon, in a short time
Swoon, to faint
Star-ling, a singing bird
Ster-ling, genuine, proved

T

Ten-or, a sound in music
Ten-ure, right of holding
Tile, a plate of baked clay
Toil, to labor
Tow-er, an elevated building
Tour, a travel, a journey

U

Un-do, to take apart
Un-due, not right, not legal

V

Val-ley, space between hills
Val-ue, the worth of a thing

W

Wan-der, to ramble about
Won-der, astonishment
Which, this or that
Witch, an artful woman
Wheth-er, which of the two
Whith-er, to what place
Wrath, anger, rage
Wroth, angry, displeased

Y

Yarn, spun wool
Yearn, to feel pity

CHAPTER XXVIII. TWENTY-EIGHTH.

SOMETIMES A LETTER OR A PART OF A WORD STANDS FOR A WHOLE WORD AS IN THE FOLLOWING TABLE.

A. B. Bachelor of Arts
A. C. Before Christ
Acct. Account
A. D. in the year of our Lord
A. M. Master of Arts, Fore-noon, In the year of the world
Anon. Without a name
Bart. Baronet
B. D. Bachelor of Divinity
Bp. Bishop
C. Cent. A hundred
Chap. Chapter
Co. Company or County

Cr. Creditor
Cwt. Hundred-weight
D. Five hundred
D. D. Doctor of Divinity
Do. Ditto, The same
Dol. Dollar
Dr. Debtor: Doctor
E. G. For Example
Etc. Et cetera, and the rest
Ed. Editor
Exr. Executor
Esq. Esquire
F. R. S. Fellow of the Royal Society
Fla. Florida
Fol. Folio
Gent. Gentleman
Gov. Governor
Hhd. Hogshead
H. B. M. Her Britannic Majesty
Hon. Honorable
I. e. that is
Ib. Ibid, In the same place
Id. Idem, The same
I. H. S. Jesus the Savior of men
Inst. Instant
Incog. Unknown
J. P. Justice of the Peace
Kt. Knight
LL. D. Doctor of Literary Laws
L. S. Place of the Seal
L. S. D. Pounds, shillings, and pence
La. Louisiana
Lib. Book
Lieut. Lieutenant
M. B. Bachelor of Medicine
M. D. Doctor of Medicine
Mr. Master, or Mister
Mrs. Mistress
Messrs. Gentlemen, Sirs
MSS. Manuscripts
M. Meridian, Noon
M. One thousand
Maj. Major
M. C. Member of Congress
M. P. Member of Parliament
Mo. Missouri
MDCCCL. Eighteen hundred and fifty (1850)
N. B. Note, or observe well
Nem. Con. No one opposing
No. Number
N. S. New Style (1752)
N. E. New England
O. S. Old Style
Oz. Ounce
P. M. Afternoon
P. S. Written after
Per Cent. By the hundred
Prox. Proximo, The next
P. Page, pp. Pages
Q. E. D. Which was to be proved
Q. V. Which see
Rev. Reverend; Revelation
S. South; Shilling
St. Saint
S. T. P. Professor of Divinity
U. S. A. United States of America
Ult. Ultimo, The last
Vs. Versus, Against
Vide, See
Vol. Volume
&, and

CHAPTER XXIX. TWENTY-NINTH.

IN THIS CHAPTER THE CHILD MAY LEARN THE ITALIC ALPHABET.

A a was an *apple* for Aaron to eat—
B b was a *boxer* for bullies to beat:
C c was a *Christian* resigned to his fate—
D d was a *drunkard* who spent his estate:
E e was an *Englishman* hunting for gold—
F f was a *Frenchman*, gay, gallant, and bold:
G g was a *gentleman* learned and polite—
H h was a *huntsman* who rode out of sight:
I i was an *Indian* who painted his face—
J j was a *jockey* without money or grace
K k was a *kite* that flew high in the air—
L l was a *lapdog* caressed by the fair:
M m was a *monkey* that came over the sea—
N n was a *negro* who sighed to be free:
O o was an *oyster* that lived upon brine—
P p was a *pumpkin* which grew on a vine:
Q q was a *quaker* who always loved peace—
R r was *religion* which makes sorrows cease:
S s was a *sailor* that launched from the shore—
T t was a *traveller* all the world o'er
U u was a *unicorn* that strove for the crown—
V v was a *vineyard* which cheer'd the whole town:
W w was as wise as a letter could be—
X x was a *Xenophon* wiser than he:
Y y was a *youth* who was honest and good—
Z z was a *zebra* that lived in a wood.

CHAPTER XXX. THIRTIETH.

PROVERBS.

1. All is well that ends well. Art improves nature.
A good man is a wise man. A weaver will weave.
Buy the truth and sell it not. Beware of flattery.
Bounty creates esteem. Bridle your tongue.
2. Correction betimes prevents many crimes.
Children are certain cares, but uncertain comforts.
Diligence gains time. Delay is dangerous.
Death is unavoidable. Death levels all.
3. Ever drink, ever dry. Envy punishes itself.
Even a fool, if he holds his tongue, may be thought wise
Fair and easy goes far. Fortune is blind.
Fat paunches, lean plates. Fear attends vice.
4. Gentleness begets friends. Good words cost nought.
Give an inch and take an ell. Gifts catch men.
He plays best who wins. Hope well and have well.
Hope keeps the heart whole. Honor good men.
5. Trust before you try—repent before you die.
If pride were a deadly disease, how many would die.
If life could be bought, the rich would live long.
Ill news will come too soon. Idleness begets vice.
6. Knowledge is no burden. Kissing goes by favor.
Keep sacred your promise. Knowledge is a treasure.
Look before you leap. Like father like son.
Little said soon mended. Love me little, love me long.
7. Money moves all. Many men of many minds.
Much coin much care. Manners make the man.
Nothing venture, nothing have. New lords, new laws.
Nought is never in danger. Nature is various.

8. Out of sight out of mind. One fool makes many.
Of two evils, choose the least. Opportunity makes a thief.
Promise with caution. Pay with punctuality.
Pardon others, but not thyself. Pride must fall.
9. Reward sweetens labor. Respect is due to age.
Reprove thy friend, correct thyself. Reveal no secrets
Soon hot, soon cold. Study makes men humane.
Stolen waters are sweet. Speak evil of none.
10. The best may mend. Two eyes see more than one.
The tree is known by its fruit. Time eases grief.
Virtue alone is happiness below. Unite and be free.
Vices come of idleness. Understanding gains favor.
11. Win gold and wear it. Wise men are scarce.
When it rains porridge, hold up your dish.
Youth wants experience. Yield to your betters.
Zeal for the truth should be cherished in youth.

CHAPTER XXXI. THIRTY-FIRST.

AGAINST QUARRELLING.

1. Charles, here are more stories for you. Stories about good boys and naughty boys, and silly boys, for you know now what it is to be good. And there is a story about two foolish cocks that were always quarrelling: and that you know is very naughty.

2. You do not quarrel! No: I am glad of it: but if you see any little boys that do quarrel, you may tell them.

THE STORY OF THE TWO COCKS.

3. There was once a hen that lived in a farm-yard, and she had a large brood of chickens. She took great care of them, and gathered them under her wings every

night, and fed them, and nursed them very well, and they were good chickens, all except two cocks, that were always quarrelling with one another.

4. These two cocks were hardly out of the shell, before they began to pick at each other; and when they grew bigger, they fought till they were all bloody. If one picked up a barley-corn, or a grain of wheat, the other always wanted to have it. They never looked pretty, because their feathers were pulled off in fighting till they were quite bare, and they picked at one another's eyes till they were both almost blind.

5. The old hen very often told them how naughty it was to quarrel so; but they did not mind her, and that you know was very naughty. So one day these two cocks had been fighting, as they always did; and the biggest cock, whose name was Chanticleer, beat the other, and crowed over him, and drove him quite out of the yard.

6. The cock that had been beat, slunk away and hid himself, for he was very much vexed to think he had been conquered, and he wanted sadly to be revenged; but he did not know how to manage it, for he was not strong enough himself.

7. So after thinking a great deal, he went to an old sly fox, that lived near, and said to him, Fox, if you will come with me, I will show you where there is a large fat cock in a farm-yard, and you may eat him up if you will.

8. The fox was very glad, for he was hungry enough; and he said, Yes, I will come directly, with all my heart, and I will not leave a feather of him. So they went together, and the cock showed Reynard the way into the farm-yard; and there was poor Chanticleer, fast asleep upon the perch. And the fox seized him by the neck, and eat him up; while the other cock stood by, and crowed for joy.

9. But when the fox had done, he said, Chanticleer was very good, but I have not had enough; I think I must try how you taste; so he flew upon the other cock, and eat him up in a moment.

CHAPTER XXXII. THIRTY-SECOND.

1. Now I will tell you a story about a very naughty boy, who loved quarrelling, and would not quit till he had killed his brother:—and this is it.

2. Adam and Eve had two sons, Cain and Abel. Cain was a very naughty quarrelsome boy; but Abel was a very good friendly boy, and God loved him very much, because he was good. But nobody loved Cain, he was so ill-natured and quarrelsome.

3. These two brothers grew up and became men. Cain was always trying to vex his brother Abel, and to make him quarrel: but Abel said, No, why should we quarrel? we are brothers, and we had much better live in peace. If we are friendly and love one another, we shall make our good parents happy, and be happy ourselves.

4. Cain would not take the good advice of his brother Abel; but was wroth. "And it came to pass, while they were in the field together, that Cain rose up against Abel his brother, and slew him.

5. And God said unto Cain, Where is Abel, thy brother? and he said, I know not. Am I my brother's keeper? And God said, What hast thou done? The voice of thy brother's blood crieth out unto me from the ground.

6. And now art thou cursed from the earth, which hath opened her mouth to receive thy brother's blood at thy hand. When thou tillest the ground, it shall not henceforth yield its fruit: thorns and thistles shall it

bring forth unto thee, and thou shalt be a fugitive and a vagabond in the earth.

7. And Cain said unto the Lord, My punishment is greater than I can bear. Behold, thou hast driven me out this day from the face of the earth; and from thy face shall I be hid: and I shall be a fugitive and a vagabond in the earth: and it shall come to pass, that every one that findeth me, shall slay me. So he went out from the presence of the Lord."

8. Whatever brawls disturb the street,
There should be peace at home:
Where sisters dwell and brothers meet,
Quarrels should never come.

9. Birds in their little nests agree,
And tis a shameful sight,
When children of one family
Fall out, and chide, and fight.

10. The devil tempts one mother's son
To rage against another;
So wicked Cain was hurried on
Till he had killed his brother.

11. Pardon, O Lord! our childish rage;
Our little brawls remove:
That as we grow to riper age,
Our hearts may all be love.

CHAPTER XXXIII. THIRTY-THIRD.

TOM NODDY AND HIS SISTER SUE,

Two Undutiful Children.

1 Tom was a very pretty boy, and his sister a very pretty girl to look on; but they were both so naughty that they would seldom do as they were bid, and were so obstinate as not to take good advice.

2. One day, as they were driving about the cows in the field by the house, their mamma bid them come in before they were hurt; and told them, if they did not take care, the cows would hook them with their horns: however, they did not mind what she said, and that you know was very naughty and very wicked.

3. Just as their mother had called them, a hawk flew over the field: which a hen observing, she called her chickens, and they all ran immediately under her wings for shelter; and by that means were secure from the voracious hawk, who would otherwise have eaten them up.

4. Upon which a gentleman who stood by, called to the children—Look ye here, Tommy, and see here, Sukey, said he, these chickens, though they are so little, have more sense than you; for they know that their mother is older and wiser than they, and therefore they always do as she bids them.

5. When the hen saw the hawk hovering in the air, to pick up her chickens, she called them, and they readily ran under her wings; but when your mother saw you in danger of being hurt by the cows, you would not go to her, though she called you again and again.

6. Ah! I don't care, what do you think I mind you? says Tom: I don't care, what do you think I mind you? says Sue: and away they both scampered after the cattle

7. The gentleman, who heard the bull grumble, and saw him curl up his ugly face, called to them again, and

ran to bring them back; but before he could get near them, the bull with his horns had tost them both into the air; and the cows, when they fell, trampled them in the dirt.

8. And what became of this naughty boy and girl afterwards, I do not know: but this I know, that all boys and girls who are not dutiful and obedient to their parents, never come to any good, but are, as they ought to be, always neglected and despised.

9. All dutiful children who do as they are bid,
Shall be loved, and applauded, and never be chid,
And their friends, and their fame, and their wealth shall increase,
Till they're crowned with the blessings of plenty and peace.

CHAPTER XXXIV. THIRTY-FOURTH.

DUTY TO PARENTS.

1. Solomon saith, "The eye that mocketh at his father, and refuseth to obey his mother, the ravens of

the valley shall pick it out, and the young eagles shall eat it."

2. The law of God, in the twentieth chapter of Leviticus, is thus—"Every one that curseth his father or his mother, shall surely be put to death: his blood shall be upon his head."

3. The fifth commandment is, Honor thy father and thy mother, that thy days may be long in the land which the Lord thy God giveth thee.

4. Go to the desert, my son, observe the young stork of the wilderness, let him speak to thy heart: he beareth on his wings his aged sire, he lodgeth him in safety, and supplieth him with food.

5. Be grateful then to thy father, for he gave thee life, and to thy mother, for she sustaineth thee. Hear the words of his mouth, for they are spoken for thy good; give ear to her admonition, for it proceedeth from love.

6. Thy father hath watched for thy welfare, he hath toiled for thy ease; do honor therefore to his age, and let not his gray hairs go down with sorrow to the grave.—Thy mother loved thee when thou wast a child; therefore when she is old, indulge her infirmities; assist and support her in the decline of life.

Let children that would fear the Lord,
  Hear what their teachers say;
With reverence meet their parents' word,
  And with delight obey.

CHAPTER XXXV. THIRTY-FIFTH.

Who is my neighbor? Luke x. 30—37.

1. A certain man went down from Jerusalem to Jericho, and fell among thieves, which stripped him of

his raiment, and wounded him, and departed, leaving him half dead.

2. And by chance there came down a certain priest that way; and when he saw him, he passed by on the one side. And likewise a Levite, when he was at the place, came and looked on him, and passed by on the other side.

3. But a certain Samaritan, as he journeyed, came where he was; and when he saw him, he had compassion on him, and went to him, and bound up his wounds, pouring in oil and wine, and set him on his own beast, and brought him to an inn, and took care of him.

4. And on the morrow, when he departed, he took out two-pence and gave them to the host, and said unto him, Take care of him; and whatsoever thou spendest more, when I come again, I will repay thee.

5. Which now of these three, thinkest thou, was neighbor unto him that fell among the thieves? And he said, He that showeth mercy unto him. Then said Jesus unto him, Go, and do thou likewise.

CHAPTER XXXVI. THIRTY-SIXTH.

THE THREE LITTLE BOYS, AND THEIR THREE CAKES.

1. There was a little boy, whose name was Harry, and his papa and mamma sent him to school.—Now Harry was a clever fellow, and loved his book, and he got to be first in his class.

2. So his mamma got up one morning very early, and called Betty the maid, and said, Betty, I think we must make a cake for Harry, for he has learned his lesson very well. And Betty said, Yes, with all my heart.

3. So they made a nice cake: it was very large, and stuffed full of plums, sweetmeats, orange and citron;

and it was iced all over with sugar: it was white and smooth on the top like snow; and this cake was sent to school.

4. When little Harry saw the cake, he was very glad, and jumped about for joy, and he hardly staid for a knife to cut a piece, but gnawed it like a little dog.

5. So he ate till the bell rang for school, and after school he ate again, and ate till he went to bed: nay, his bed-fellow told me he laid his cake under his pillow, and sat up in the night to eat some. And he ate, and ate, till it was all gone.

6. But presently after, this little boy was very sick and ill, and every body said, I wonder what is the matter with Harry! he used to be so brisk, and play about more nimbly than any of the boys; but now he looks pale, and is very ill.

7. And somebody said, Harry had a rich cake, and he ate it up very soon, and that has made him ill. So they sent for Dr. Camomile, and he gave him, I do not know how much bitter stuff. Poor Harry did not like it at all; it was a bitter pill, but the Doctor said he must take it; or else he would have died, you know. However, at last he got well again; but his mamma said she would send him no more cakes.

8. Now there was another boy, who was one of Harry's school-fellows; his name was Peter—the boys used to call him Peter Careful. And Peter had written his mamma a very neat, pretty letter—there was not one blot in it all. So his mamma sent him a cake.

9. Now Peter thought with himself, I will not be so silly as to make myself sick with this good cake, as Harry did; I will keep it a great while. So he took the cake, and tugged it up stairs: it was heavy: he could hardly carry it.

10. And he locked it up in his box, and once a day he crept slily up stairs, and ate a very little piece, and

then he locked his box again. So he kept it several weeks, and it was not gone, for it was very large:—But, behold! the mice got into his box, and nibbled some.

11. And Peter's cake grew dry, and mouldy, and at last he was obliged to throw it away; and it grieved him to the very heart, but nobody was sorry for him.

12. Well, there was another little boy at the same school, whose name was Billy: and one day his mamma sent him a cake, because she loved him dearly, and he loved her dearly. So, when the cake came, Billy said to his school-fellows, I have got a cake; come, let us go and eat it.

13. So, they came about him like a parcel of bees; and Billy took a slice of cake himself, and then gave a piece to one, and a piece to another, and a piece to another, till it was almost gone. Then Billy put the rest by, and said, We will eat this to-morrow. So he went to play, and the boys all played together very merrily.

14. But presently after, an old blind fiddler came into the yard: he had a long white beard; and because he was blind, he had a little dog in a string to lead him. So he came into the yard, and sat down upon a stone, and said, My pretty lads, if you will, I will play you a tune; and they all left off their sport, and came and stood round him.

15. And Billy saw, that while he played, the tears ran down his cheeks. And Billy said, Good man, why do you cry? And the old man said, Because I am very ungry. I have nobody to give me any dinners or suppers: I have nothing in the world but this little dog: and I cannot work. If I could work, I would.

16. Then Billy went, without saying a word, and brought the rest of the cake which he intended to have eaten the next day; and he said, Here, old man! here is some cake for you. The old man said, Where is it?

for I am blind; I cannot see it. So Billy put it into his hat.

17. And the fiddler thanked him; and Billy was more glad than if he had eaten ten cakes. Pray, which do you love best? do you love Harry, or Peter, or Billy best?

CHAPTER XXXVII. THIRTY-SEVENTH.

HOSPITALITY OF EDWIN, THE HERMIT, TO A STRANGER WHO HAD LOST HIS WAY.

1. Here to the houseless child of want,
   My door is open still;
And though my portion is but scant,
   I give it with good-will.
Then turn to-night, and freely share
   Whate'er my cell bestows:
My rushy couch and frugal fare,
   My blessings and repose.

2. No flocks that range the valleys free,
   To slaughter I condemn,
Taught by that Power that pities me,
   I learn to pity them.
But from the mountain's grassy side,
   A guiltless feast I bring;
A scrip with herbs and fruit supplied,
   And water from the spring.

3. Then, pilgrim, turn, thy cares forego,
   For earth-born cares are wrong:
Man wants but little here below,
   Nor wants that little long.
Soft as the dew from heaven descends,
   His gentle accents fell:
The grateful stranger lowly bends,
   And follows to the cell.

4. And now when worldly crowds retire,
To revels or to rest;
The Hermit trimm'd his little fire,
And cheer'd his pensive guest.
Then spread his vegetable store,
And gaily prest, and smil'd;
And, skill'd in legendary lore,
The ling'ring hours beguil'd.

CHAPTER XXXVIII. THIRTY-EIGHTH.

HE THAT GIVETH TO THE POOR, LENDETH TO THE LORD.

1. There was a poor man who was charitable to excess; for he gave away all that he had to relieve the necessities of others; choosing rather to throw himself upon Providence, than to deny an alms to any one who asked him, so long as he had any thing to bestow.

2. Being at length, by his constant liberalities, reduced to a very indigent condition, he was forced to betake himself to digging for a livelihood.

3. Yet, notwithstanding he gained his own bread by hard labor, he ceased not to show his wonted kindnesses to the poor; giving them whatever he could possibly spare from his own necessities.

4. One day, as he was digging in the field, he found several earthen pots of gold, supposed to be buried there in the time of the wars. The good man carried this huge treasure home to his house, with all imaginable privacy.

5. And having distributed the greatest part of it in charity, he was going with the last reserve to the house of a distressed widow, to whom he gave a sufficient sum to relieve her wants, being all he had left: when as he

was returning home, he found a jewel in the high-way, which being sold, yielded him ten thousand crowns.

6. This was a noble bank for new liberalities, and a convincing argument, that there was something more than mere chance which thus strangely recruited his purse; that it might not lack something to give to the poor.

7. Blest is the man whose bowels move,
And melt with pity to the poor;
Whose soul with sympathizing love,
Feels what his fellow-saints endure.
His heart contrives, for their relief,
More good than his own hands can do:
He, in the time of general grief,
Shall find the Lord hath bowels too.
8. His soul shall live secure on earth,
With secret blessings on his head,
When drought, and pestilence, and dearth,
Around him multiply their dead.
Or if he languish on his couch,
God will pronounce his sins forgiv'n,
Will save him with a healing touch
Or take his willing soul to heaven.

CHAPTER XXXIX. THIRTY-NINTH.

CHARITY COVERETH A MULTITUDE OF SINS.

1. Blessed is the man that considereth the poor; the Lord will deliver him in the time of trouble. The Lord will preserve him, and keep him alive; he shall be blessed upon the earth—and Thou wilt not deliver him unto the will of his enemies.

2. There is Faith, Hope, and Charity; but the greatest of these is CHARITY.—The poor man cried, and the

Lord heard him, yea, and delivered him—Cast thy bread upon the waters, thou shalt find it after many days——If thine enemy be hungry, give him bread——He that oppresseth the poor, he also shall cry himself and not be heard.

3. Give of your portion to the poor,
   As riches do arise;
And from the needy naked soul,
   Turn not away your eyes—
God hath given you increase,
   And blessed well your store;
Remember you are put in trust,
   And should relieve the poor.

CHAPTER XL. FORTIETH.

THE LAST JUDGMENT.

1. The God of glory sends his summons forth,
Calls the south nations, and awakes the north:
From east to west the sovereign orders spread,
Through distant worlds and regions of the dead:
The trumpet sounds; hell trembles—heaven rejoices:
Lift up your heads, ye saints, with cheerful voices.

2. No more shall *atheists* mock his long delay;
His vengeance sleeps no more—behold the day!
Behold the JUDGE descends! His guards are nigh;
Tempests and fire attend him down the sky:
When God appears, all nature shall adore him:
While sinners tremble, saints rejoice before him.

3. Then shall the King say unto them on his right hand, *Come ye blessed of my Father, inherit the kingdom prepared for you from the foundation of the world:* For I was an hungered, and ye gave me meat: I was thirsty, and ye gave me drink; I was a stranger, and ye took

me in; I was naked, and ye clothed me; I was sick, and ye visited me; I was in prison, and ye came unto me.

4. Then shall the righteous answer him, saying, Lord, when saw we thee an hungered, and fed thee? Or thirsty, and gave thee drink? When saw we thee a stranger, and took thee in? Or naked, and clothed thee? Or when saw we thee sick or in prison, and came unto thee?

5. And the King shall answer, and say unto them; Verily I say unto you, inasmuch as ye have done it unto the least of these my brethren, ye have done it unto me.

6. Then shall he say also unto them on the left hand, *Depart from me, ye cursed, into everlasting fire, prepared for the devil and his angels:* For I was an hungered, and ye gave me no meat; I was thirsty, and ye gave me no drink; I was a stranger, and ye took me not in; naked, and ye clothed me not; sick, and in prison, and ye visited me not.

7. Then shall they also answer him, saying, Lord, when saw we thee an hungered, or athirst, or a stranger, or naked, or sick, or in prison, and did not minister unto thee?

8. Then shall he answer them, saying, Verily, I say unto you, inasmuch as ye did it not to one of the least of these, ye did it not to me: And these shall go away into everlasting punishment, but the righteous into life eternal.

DESCRIPTION OF A GOOD BOY.

1. A good boy is dutiful to his father and mother, obedient to his master, and loving to all his play-fellows: and is diligent in learning his book, and takes a pleasure in improving himself in every thing that is worthy of praise.

2. He rises early in the morning, makes himself clean and decent, and says his prayers. If he has done a fault, he confesses it, and is sorry for it, and scorns to tell a lie, though he might by that means conceal it.

3. He loves to hear good advice, is thankful to those that give it him, and always follows it. He never swears, nor calls names, nor uses any ill words to his companions. He is never peevish nor fretful, but always cheerful and good-humored.

4. He scorns to steal or pilfer any thing from his play-fellows; and would rather suffer wrong, than do wrong to any of them. He is always ready to answer when he is asked a question, to do what he is bid, and to mind what is said to him. He is not a wrangler, nor quarrelsome, and keeps himself out of all kinds of mischief which other boys run into.

5. By this means he becomes, as he grows up, a man of sense and virtue; he is beloved and respected by all that know him; he lives in the world with credit and reputation, and when he dies, is lamented by all his acquaintance.

DESCRIPTION OF A BAD BOY.

6. A bad boy is undutiful to his father and mother, disobedient and stubborn to his master, and ill-natured

to all his play-fellows. He hates his book, and takes no pleasure in improving himself in any thing. He is sleepy and slothful in the morning, too idle to clean himself, and too wicked to say his prayers.

7. He is always in mischief, and when he has done a fault, will tell twenty lies in hopes to clear himself, which is only making bad worse. He hates that any body should give him good advice, and when they are out of sight, will laugh at them. He swears and wrangles, and quarrels with his companions, and is always in some dispute or other.

8. He will steal whatsoever comes in his way: and if he is not catched, thinks it no crime, not considering that God sees whatsoever he does. He is frequently out of humor, and sullen, and obstinate, so that he will neither do what he is bid, nor answer any question that is asked him.

9. In short, he neglects every thing that he should learn, and minds nothing but play or mischief; by which means he becomes, as he grows up, a confirmed block-head, incapable of any thing but wickedness, or folly, despised by all men of sense and virtue, and generally dies a beggar.

CHAPTER XLI. FORTY-FIRST.

THE BOY THAT WENT TO THE WOOD TO LOOK FOR BIRDS' NESTS, WHEN HE SHOULD HAVE GONE TO SCHOOL.

1. When Jack got up, and put on his clothes, he thought if he could get to the wood, he should be quite well: for the poor fool thought more of a bird-nest than he did of his book, that would make him wise and great.

2. When he came there, he found no nest but one, that was on the top of a tree, and with much ado, he

gets up to it, and robs it of its eggs. Then he tries to get down, but a branch of the tree found a hole in the skirt of his coat, and held him fast.

3. At this time, he would have been glad to have been at school; for the bird, in a rage at the loss of her eggs, flew at him, and was like to pick out his eyes. Now it was that the sight of a man at the foot of the tree gave him more joy than all the nests in the wood.

4. This man was so kind as to chase away the bird, and help him out of the tree; and from that time forth, he would not loiter from school, and had the praise and good-will of all that knew him.

CHAPTER XLII. FORTY-SECOND.

ADVANTAGE OF LEARNING TO READ.

1. The knowledge of letters, saith Dr. Watts, is the greatest blessing that God ever bestowed upon man. By this means we preserve, for our own use through all our lives, what our memory would have lost in a few days; and lay up a rich treasure of knowledge for those that come after us.

2. By the art of reading and writing we can sit at home, and acquaint ourselves with what is done in all

the distant parts of the world, and find what our fathers did long ago, in the first ages of mankind.

3. By this means a Briton holds a correspondence with his friend, in America, or Japan, and manages all his traffic. We learn, by this means, how the old Romans lived, how the Jews worshipped; we learn what Moses wrote, what Enoch prophesied, where Adam dwelt, and what he did soon after the creation.

4. And those who live when the day of judgment comes, may learn, by the same means, what we now speak, and what is done in Great Britain, or in the land of China.

5. In short, the art of letters does, as it were, revive all the past ages of men, and set them at once on the stage, and brings all the nations from afar, and gives them, as it were, a general interview; so that the most distant nations, and distant ages of mankind, may converse together, and grow into acquaintance.

6. But the greatest blessing of all, is the knowledge of the Holy Scriptures, wherein God hath appointed his servants, in ancient times, to write down the discoveries which he hath made of his power and justice, his provi-

dence and grace, that we who live near the end of time, may learn the way to heaven, and everlasting happiness.

7. Thus, letters give us a sort of Immortality in this world, and they have given us the word of God, to support our immortal hope in the world to come.

8. The youth who led by Wisdom's guiding hand,
Seeks VIRTUE's temple, and her law reveres;
He, he alone, in HONOR's dome shall stand,
Crown'd with REWARDS, and rais'd above his peers;
Recording annals shall preserve his NAME,
And give his virtues to immortal FAME.

CHAPTER XLIII. FORTY-THIRD.

THE REWARD OF VIRTUE.

1. Piety, modesty, and a tender, generous heart, are much greater ornaments than fine clothes; for the good are always admired, praised, and beloved; the good are happy: God is their friend, and is invariably disposed by nature to reward their virtue.

2. How happy are those children who have God for their friend! they have nothing to fear; they may smile in death, and leave this world with pleasure.

3. Miss Goodchild had the advantage of such instruction in her youth, that she could reason justly on the obligation of virtue; the being of providence and perfections of God; whom she admired, loved, and revered, from a conviction of his infinite excellencies; and to whom, every morning and evening, she offered up her prayers for protection, and for advancement in useful knowledge, and good dispositions, the chief object of her pursuit.

4. Her papa and mamma soon died, and she had no other portion left, but her undissembled piety; a decent modesty, which showed itself in all her actions, an in-

nocent simplicity, and a heart full of goodness: these raised her friends, who admired her, and strove to make her happy.

5. A gentleman of understanding and virtue became sensible of her merit, and married her. It was the business of their lives to make each other happy: and as their fortune was large, she was enabled to gratify the generous dispositions of her heart, in relieving the necessities of the poor, and in using the power which her riches gave her, in promoting the happiness of all about her.

6. Mylo! forbear to call him blest,
 Who only boasts a large estate:
Should all the treasures of the West,
 Meet, and conspire to make him great.
I know thy better thoughts, I know,
Thy reason can't descend so low.
Let a broad stream, with golden sands,
 Through all his meadows roll,
He's but a wretch, with all his lands,
 Who wears a narrow soul.

CHAPTER XLIV. FORTY-FOURTH.

THE ADVICE OF WILLIAM PENN, TO HIS CHILDREN.

My Dear Children,

1. Not knowing how long it may please God to continue me among you, I am willing to embrace this opportunity of leaving you my advice, with respect to your duty in this world:—And I do beseech you, and charge you, by the relation you have to me, and the affection which I have always shown to you, and indeed received from you, that you lay up the same in your hearts, with a wise and religious care.

2. I will begin with that which is the beginning of knowledge, *The Fear of the Lord.*

3. Children! fear God; that is, have an holy awe upon your minds, to avoid that which is evil, and a strict care to embrace and do that which is good:—the measure and standard of which knowledge and duty is the Word of God, and the light of your consciences.

4. This knowledge is the *pearl of great price;* the divine and incorruptible seed of the kingdom of Heaven. Receive it into your hearts; give it room there; let it take deep root in you, and you will be fruitful unto God, in every good word and work.

5. There is no other virtue or power, that will carry you through the world to God's glory, or your own everlasting peace.

6. Your most tender father prays, that you may be kept in the faith and practice of this blessed testimony: and you should count it no small mercy from God, and honor to yourselves, that you came of parents, who counted nothing too great to do or suffer, that they might approve themselves to God, and testify their love to his most precious truth.

7. In the morning, when you awake, let your minds retire into a pure silence from all worldly things; and in that frame, wait upon God; to feel his good presence; to lift up your heart to him, and commit your whole self to his blessed care and protection.

8. When you rise, read a chapter in the Bible; and then dispose yourselves for the business of the day; ever remembering, that God is present, the overseer of all our thoughts, words and actions; and behave yourselves, my dear children, accordingly: and do not dare to do that in his holy presence, which ye would be ashamed to do before men.

9. In conversation, mark well what others say, and hide your own mind, till a fair opportunity offers; and

then open it as sparingly as the matter will let you. Just observations and reflections upon men and things, give wisdom; those are the great books of learning, which are too seldom read.

10. The laborious bee draws honey from every flower. Be always on your guard, especially in company; then be sure to have your wits about you, and your armor on. *Be quick to hear, and slow to speak.* Speak little, but when you do speak, let it be to the point: and when you have nothing to say, *say nothing.*

11. Prefer the aged, the virtuous, and the knowing, and choose those who excel in goodness, for your company and friendship.

12. Reason not with an angry man: it is then a wrong time to convince him, or to vindicate yourself. When men are angry, they are not themselves, and know not what spirits they are of. Wait till he is cool, and then he will hear you.

13. Be *plain* in your clothes, and in your furniture, and in your food: but be *clean.*

14. Have few acquaintances and fewer intimates: but the best of their kind.

15. Keep your own secrets; but do not covet others: yet, if you are intrusted, never reveal them, unless they are mischievous.

16. Trust no man with the *main chance;* and avoid being trusted.

17. Make few promises, but keep them strictly.

18. Prefer *elders* and *strangers* on all occasions.

19. Have a care of trusting *to-morrow.* Wisdom is beforehand, and teaches us to choose seasonably, and pertinently; therefore ever *strike while the iron is hot.*

20. Have few books; but let them be well chosen, and well read.

21. Do not do that to another, which you would not like to have another do to you.

22. Love one another; and remember, that to be void of natural affection, is a mark of apostacy.

23. The wisdom of nations lies in their Proverbs: collect them, and learn them.

24. Never meddle with other folks' business.

25. Have a care of *resentment;* it is a most dangerous passion; be more ready to forgive than to revenge injuries.

26. Rejoice not at the calamities of others; though they may be your enemies.

27. Envy none: it is God who maketh rich and poor, great and small, high and low.

28. Never revile, nor call ill names; it is unmannerly, as well as unchristian.

29. Love home; fear God; know yourselves; know your own business, and do it; and you will have more time and more peace than your neighbors.

30. Avoid pride as you would avoid the devil.

31. Show mercy whenever it is in your power; that is, forgive, pity, and help others.

32. Charity is a near neighbor to mercy; it consists in speaking favorably of others, and in relieving the poor; therefore, be charitable.

33. As objects of charity, I recommend to you *little children, widows, and aged persons.* Spare something from your own food, rather than let them go hungry.

34. In distributing justice, know no man, after the flesh: know neither rich, nor poor; great, nor small; kindred, nor stranger; but judge the cause according to your understanding and conscience; upon deliberate inquiry and information.

35. Integrity is a great and commendable virtue. A man of integrity, is a true man, and a steady man; he is to be trusted, and relied upon. No bribes can corrupt him, nor fear daunt him; he shines brightest in

the fire, and his friend hears of him most when he most needs him.

36. Take heed; look to your ways; have a care what you do; let your moderation be known unto all men, for the Lord is at hand.

37. And now, my dear children, let us hear the conclusion of the whole matter: Fear God, and keep his commandments, for this is the whole duty of man. For God shall bring every work into judgment with every secret thing, whether it be good or whether it be evil.

WILLIAM PENN.

CHAPTER XLV. FORTY-FIFTH.

LESSONS IN LIFE.

1. There was once such a disturbance in the state of Literature, that great *A*, who presides over the commonwealth of Letters, was obliged to summon all the members to prepare for war. He appeared in the field with little *a*, and the first that came to them was great *B*, with little *b* behind him.

2. Mr. *B*, says *A*, you are a blockhead, and little *b* is no better; how came you to be absent from church last Sunday? One who has no religion is not fit for a soldier, nor any other employment.—Then came great *C*, with little *c* behind him.

3. Mr. *C*, says *A*, you are a coxcomb, and a coward; one who fawns and cringes in your manner, I doubt has but little sincerity, and less resolution. I expect to have my company more manly, and to behave with openness and freedom.—Then came great *D*, with little *d*.

4. Mr. *D*, says he, your son is a dunce, and cannot understand me; and you are a drunkard, and not to be trusted, for a drunken man keeps no secrets, no, not

even his own; and besides, he that will barter his senses for a pot of beer, and give up his reason to gratify his depraved appetite, can have no regard for religion or morality. Go and learn to behave better.—Then came great *E*, with little *e*.

5. Mr. *E*, says he, you are ever ready to do good; ever ready to learn your book; ever ready to go to church; ever ready to relieve the poor; ever ready to assist those that are distressed, and have never once, to my knowledge, been naughty; come, and stand next to me, for you and your sons shall be officers.—Then came great *F*, with little *f*.

6. Mr. *F*, says he, you are a fop, and for aught I know, a fool; one who is so fond of himself, and spends half his time in curling his pate, as you do, can be good for little else; walk away, pray, now.—Then came great *G*, with little *g*.

7. Mr. *G*, says he, you are a gambler, and your son is a gamester: how many families have you ruined! A highwayman has not a worse character. Go along, for no such fellow shall ride in my regiment.—Then came great *H*, with little *h*.

8. Mr. *H*, says he, you are a mighty hunter, and so is your son; but I hope you do not break down the farmers' fences, and tread down their corn; if you do, I shall have nothing to say to you; therefore, stand by, till I have inquired into your character.—Then came up great *I*, with little *i*.

9. Mr. *I*, says he, I hear you are an idle fellow, and that you bring up your son in idleness. An idle man is an enemy to the nation; for he lives upon other people's labor, and does nothing for his own support. Idleness, says King Solomon, will clothe a man with rags: and I shall see you in tatters by and by: go along, sirrah.—Then came great *J*, with little *j*.

10. Mr. *J*, says he, I am told that you are a jack at

all trades, and I am afraid that you will be good at none. The man who attempts to do a great many things at once, generally does nothing as it ought to be done. One trade, well followed, is enough for one man. If you have too many irons in the fire, some of them must burn. Please to stand by, sir, and make room for great *K*, and little *k*.

11. Mr. *K*, says he, you want to be a king, I find; but you ought to consider that a crown is a cap of care. A man who is intoxicated with ambition, insensible to the cries of the distressed, and for grasping all power and riches into his own hands, is unfit for my service, or that of the public.—Then came great *L*, with little *l*.

12. Mr. *L*, says he, I find you are a lively companion, and a lover of learning: sit down by me, pray now, for such a gentleman as you, I want to enlist in my company—your cheerfulness is a sign of innocence, and your learning is better than gold, yea, better than fine gold; sweeter also than honey, and the honey-comb.—Then came great *M*, with little *m*.

13. Mr. *M*, says he, I hear you are a miser, which is a character I abhor—for a miser hoards up his gold, and renders it useless to himself and to every body else. He is like the dog in the manger, he will neither eat himself, nor suffer others to eat—go along, sirrah.—Then came great *N*, with little *n*.

14. My lord *N*, says he, I am informed that you are a nobleman: if your title is founded on virtue and merit, there is no one will honor you more, or be so much your humble servant. If you cherish religion; if you comfort the distressed; if you assist the poor; if you strive to promote the happiness of mankind, and the good of your country; if so, you are truly noble; but if not, your nobility is but as sounding brass, or a tinkling cymbal, and has no foundation in the nature and fitness of things.—Then came great *O*, with little *o*.

15. Mr. *O*, says he, I hear you are an officious fellow; always meddling with other people's affairs, and making mischief between friends and families. Go along, sirrah, for I will have no such rascals in my regiment.—Then came great *P*, with little *p*.

16. Mr. *P*, says he, you are a prating puppy, always talking about things you do not understand: you have not sense enough to know that you are a fool; if you had, you would sometimes be silent, that you might learn. He who always talks, has no time to hear.—Then came great *Q*, with little *q*.

17. Mr. *Q*, says he, I hear you are quarrelsome; and if so, no man of sense, will keep your company; for all your companions will be involved in your difficulties, and become parties in quarrels, with which they ought to have no concern. Every man of sense will defend his own character, and countenance his friend; but no man is obliged to run his head against every blockhead he meets, because they happen to know a fool of his acquaintance.—Then came great *R*, with little *r*.

18. Mr. *R*, says he, I hear you are very rich; but that is not to me a sufficient recommendation; for, as a rich man may be a great rogue, and has it in his power to do more mischief than one of the same disposition, who is not so wealthy; I must know how you employ your riches before you can ride in my regiment.—Then came great *S*, with little *s*.

19. Mr. *S*, says he, you are a spendthrift; you have squandered away your estate, and neglected your own affairs, and how can I expect you will take care of mine? Walk along, sir.—Then came great *T*, with little *t*.

20. Mr. *T*, says he, I hear you are a thief, and if you do not clear yourself of this charge, I shall neither admit you into my house, nor into my regiment. A thief is the most despicable of all characters: I would not, for the whole world, have a single one in my company: *for one*

scabby sheep will spoil a whole flock.—Then came great *U*, with little *u*.

21. Mr. *U*, says he, I am informed you are a great usurer; that you extort the most extravagant interest from honest tradesmen, who are in distress; that you have no compassion on the needy, and that you grind the face of the poor. If these things be true, I shall consider all your pretences to religion, only as vile cloaks for your sins. A hypocrite in religion, is hateful, both to God and man.—Then came great *V*, with little *v*.

22. Mr. *V*, says he, I hear you are a great vaunter, and boast even of actions that you have never attempted. A braggadocio is always a coward; besides, you have no regard for truth—and who would connect himself with a liar? Truth is so divine, so desirable, that all wise and good men are in the search of it—but lying lips, who can bear? all liars shall have their part in the lake that burns with fire and brimstone.—Then came great *W*, with little *w*.

23. Mr. *W*, says he, I rejoice to see you well. I take you to my heart, and shall always esteem a friend like you, as an invaluable treasure. You are not only wise, but you are good—for he that has true wisdom, must, I think, have innate goodness. You are constant and steady in the worship of the Almighty—and before him, offer up the most grateful of all sacrifices; that of an upright heart. You consider every child of sorrow, as your brother—your benevolence is extended to all—though preference is given to the most industrious and deserving—you assist the fatherless, and comfort the widow—by you, the naked are clothed, and the hungry are not sent empty away—for which, the Almighty will pour down blessings on you seventy fold—Peace shall be established in your possessions, and sportive liberty shall wanton in your plains—" The clouds shall drop fatness on your fields, and the valleys shall stand so thick

with corn, that they shall laugh and sing."—Then came great *X*, with little *x*.

24. Mr. *X*, says he, you are an excellent fellow, and to you I have no exception—your learning is very extensive, and your virtues highly extolled. Your father planted in you those seeds of learning and knowledge, which grow for the good of mankind—and in you, we behold the blessed fruits of a virtuous education.—Then came great *Y*, with little *y* behind him.

25. Mr. *Y*, says he, you are young, and unfit for me at present, but if you will have a little patience, and pay attention to the useful lessons which are given you, by those who have the care of your education, you may, by and by, stand first in the rank of honor—and if you follow the advice of your most excellent father, your pursuits will be crowned with peace and plenty. For, though I have been young, and now I am old, yet never saw I the righteous forsaken, or his seed begging bread.—Then came great *Z*, and little *z* with him.

26. Mr. *Z*, says he, I know you are very zealous; but your zeal is sometimes misplaced, and then it becomes a bad ingredient, even in a good man. You ought to take care that your zeal be founded on knowledge, and consistent with humanity; otherwise, you may do more harm than those who have a worse heart. We have seen what havoc mistaken zeal has made in the world; whole nations have been ruined by it, and many people have been burnt alive. So it may be truly said, that *zeal without knowledge, is a fire without light.*

Given under my hand and seal, in the *Critic's Palace*, this 27th day of September, in the year of the world, 5792.

GREAT A.

N. B. Here you will observe that great A, being a person of prudence and penetration, never takes up with appearances only; but inspects, as it were, the very hearts of men, before he engages them in his service; for every man's disposition may be pretty well known, by comparing his words and actions for a long series of time. He had but three, as you will find, out of the whole twenty-six—a sad sign of depravity. By his example, however, and good management, all the rest were converted, and became good.

CHAPTER XLVI. FORTY-SIXTH.

A CHAPTER OF PROVERBS.

1. A proverb is a child of experience.
All the wit in the world is not in the head.
A wise man hath more ballast than sail.
A friend is not so soon found as lost.
A bird in the hand is worth two in the bush.
A fool and his money are soon parted.
2. Better spare at the brim than at the bottom.
Bought wit is best; if not bought too dear.
Better to play at small game than stand idle.
Better is half a loaf than no bread.
Be always mindful of past favors.
Birds of a feather flock together.
3. Cheer up, man, God is still where he was.
Crosses are ladders which lead to heaven.
Craft brings nothing home at last.
Covetous men's *chests* are rich, not themselves.
Conscience is a thousand witnesses.
Choose a wife on Saturday, not on Sunday.
4. Diligence will overcome difficulties.
Do no ill, and fear no harm.
Death is the doctor that cures all disorders.
Discontent is man's worst evil.

Do all you can, to be good, and you will be so.
Discretion is the parent of virtue.
5. Every bird thinks its own young the best.
Every fool is wise in his own conceit.
Every one should sweep before his own door.
Evil be to him, who evil thinks.
Every bean has its black.
Enough is as good as a feast.
6. Fair words butter no parsnips.
Fine sense is not so good as common sense.
Fly the pleasure that will bite to-morrow.
Friends do not grow on every bough.
Foolish tongues talk by the dozen.
Fierceness is softened by mildness.
7. Good to begin well, better to end well.
Good swimmers are drowned at last.
Good looks buy nothing in the market.
Great fires may be kindled with small coals.
Gold goes in any gate except heaven's.
Good husbandry is good divinity.
8. Hear with both ears, and then judge.
He looks one way, and rows the other.
He that will not work, should not eat.
He who once hits will be always shooting.
He who abounds in words, wants wit.
Honesty is the best policy—the world over.
9. If once a man fall, all will tread on him.
Idleness will clothe a man with rags.
I speak of chalk, and you of cheese.
It is a good horse that never stumbles.
It is an ill wind that blows nobody good.
I will go warm, and let fools laugh on.
10. John Do-little is the son of Sue Spin-little.
Jack will never make a gentleman.
Jealousy has a thousand eyes.

Joe's mother-wit is better than school-logic.
Jack at all trades, and good at none.

11. Keep your mouth shut, and your eyes open.
Keep thy shop, and that will keep thee.
Kings may conquer armies, but not death.
Knowledge is good for nothing unless it be used.
Keep bad company at a distance.
Keep with good men, and add to their number.

12. Lean liberty is better than fat slavery.
Lend and lose my money, so play fools.
Live, and let live: i. e. be a good landlord.
Look not a gift horse in the mouth.
Lawyers' houses are built with fools' money.
Lazy folks take the most pains.

13. Many words will not fill a bushel.
Mettle is dangerous in a blind horse.
Much better lose a jest than a friend.
Marry in haste, and repent at leisure.
Make no friendship with a bad man.
Money is a good servant, but a bad master.

14. Necessity is the mother of invention.
Never let go a certainty for an uncertainty.
Near is my shirt, but nearer is my skin.
None is a fool always; every one sometimes.
Nothing is commendable that is not just.
No ill befalls us but may be for our good.

15. One ill example spoils many good laws.
Obstinacy is the most incurable of all sins.
Oil, and truth, will get uppermost at last.
Of sinful pleasures, repentance only remains.
One fool in one house is quite enough.
Old birds, boy, are not to be caught with chaff.

16. Peace with heaven is the best friendship.
Pride goes before, and shame follows after.
Prayer and provender hinder no journey.
Penny in pocket is a good companion.

Poor folks' words answer but little purpose.
Prudence saves us from many a misfortune.
17. Quick promisers are slow performers.
Questions of moment require slow answers.
Quick believers need broad shoulders.
Quick to hear, slow to speak.
Quietness and peace make discord cease.
Quack doctors support grave-diggers.
18. Righteousness exalteth a nation.
Riches are often the servants of vice.
Rich men seem happy, great men wise.
Riches are but the baggage of virtue.
Rash anger is the author of many evils.
Rub your sore eyes with your elbows.
19. Security is the forerunner of calamity.
Saying and doing seldom dine together.
Show me a liar, and I will show you a thief.
Stay a while, that we may come the sooner.
Sin and sorrow are never far from each other.
Speak the truth and shame the devil.
20. There are more ways to the wood than one.
Those who live sinfully die sorrowfully.
Too much of one thing is good for nothing.
The best throw at dice is to throw them away.
Think much, speak little, and write less.
To err is human, to forgive, divine.
21. Use soft words and hard arguments.
Undertake great affairs with caution.
Use of a thing is the best master.
2. Vice is seldom learned without a teacher.
Value reputation more than gold.
Virtue is the best patrimony for a child.
23. While the cat sleeps, the mice skip about.
When the sky falls, we shall catch larks.
Wit once bought, is worth twice taught.
When the fox preaches, let the geese beware.

Wicked practices discover bad principles.
Wit is folly, unless a wise man possess it.

24. You have hit the nail on the head.
You can have no more of a cat than her skin.
You cannot eat your cake, and have your cake
Youth, like the spring, will soon be gone.
Young men's knocks, old men feel.
Yes, good words put off your bad ware.

25. Train up a child in the way that he should go, and when he is old he will not depart from it. Choose what is most fit; custom will make it most agreeable. Improve by other men's faults, rather than censure them.

26. As the old cock crows, the young one learns. Example is stronger than precept. Such is the father, such is the son. Children learn by imitation. Men acquire virtue or vice more from education than from nature. It is hard to teach an old dog new tricks.

27. The young are slaves to novelty, the old to custom. Custom is the plague of wise men, and the idol of fools. Superstition is the spleen of the soul. A saddle for the horse, a bridle for the ass, and a rod for the fool's back.

28. Those who set out to live by their wits, often break for want of stock. Diligence will overcome difficulties. Continual dropping will wear a stone. Little strokes fell great oaks.

29. A rolling stone will gather no moss.
I never knew an oft-removed tree,
Nor yet an oft-removed family,
That throve so well as those that settled be.

30. Three removes are as bad as a fire.

31. Seize time by the foretop. Time and tide wait for no man. Never put that off till to-morrow, which you can do to-day. A stitch in time saves nine. Lost time is never found again. What we call time enough,

always proves little enough. Make hay while the sun shines.

32. If you love life, do not waste your time, for time is the stuff life is made of. He that rises late may trot all day, and shall not be able to overtake his business at night. Drive thy work, let not that drive thee.

33. Early to bed, and early to rise, makes a man healthy, and wealthy, and wise. Diligence is the mother of success. God will help them that help themselves. Plow deep while sluggards sleep, and you shall have corn to sell and keep.

34. If you would have a good servant, serve yourself. Handle your tools without mittens. A cat in gloves catches no mice.

Many estates are spent in the getting;
Since women, for tea, forsook spinning and knitting;
And men, for punch, forsook hewing and splitting.

35. If you would be rich, think of saving, as well as earning. A penny saved is as good as a penny earned. The Indies have not made Spain rich, because her outgoes were more than her incomes.

Luxury, game, and deceit,
Make the wealth small, and the wants great.

36. What maintains one vice, will bring up two children. Beware of small expenses. Many a little makes a mickle. A small leak will sink a great ship. Fools make feasts, and great men eat them. Feasts in the parlor, put out the kitchen fire.

37. He that goes borrowing, goes sorrowing. A farmer on his legs, is higher than a gentlemen on his knees. Always taking out of the meal-tub, and never putting in, will soon come to the bottom. When money is gone, we know the want of it.

For age and want, save while you may,
No morning sun will last a whole day.

38. Pride must fall. Pride is as loud a beggar as

want, and a great deal more saucy. Pride breakfasted with plenty, dined with poverty, and supped with infamy. Cut your coat according to your cloth. Great minds and small means ruin many.

Vessels large may venture more:
But little boats should keep near shore.

39. Rather than run in debt, wear your old coat. A patch on a man's back, is not so disgraceful as a writ. Experience keeps a dear school, but fools will learn in no other. We can give advice, but we cannot give conduct. If you will not hear reason, she will surely rap your knuckles.

40. Silence is everywhere safe. Be more ready to hear than to speak. You have two ears and but one tongue, therefore you should hear twice and speak once. The prating fool shall fall. If you cannot keep your own secrets, you must not blame others for telling them.

A man of words and not of deeds,
Is like a garden full of weeds.

41. The tongue is like a race-horse; it runs faster the less weight it carries. The shallow brook warbles, while the deep water is still. An empty cask makes a great noise. Hold your tongue, and nobody will know that you are a fool. To say little and perform much, is the characteristic of a great mind. *When you have nothing to say, say nothing.*

42. Friends in need are friends indeed. Prosperity will gain friends, adversity will try them. True friends are rare: change not an old friend for a new one. If you would have friends, be friendly. One good turn deserves another. Anger resteth in the bosom of a fool. Let not the sun go down upon your wrath.

CHAPTER XLVII. FORTY-SEVENTH.

AGAINST QUARRELLING.

1. Good children do not quarrel, and hurt one another when they are at play. Naughty boys quarrel; and cats, and dogs, and wolves, and bears quarrel; but good boys live in peace: they are friendly to one another, and every body loves them.

2. Did you see the cocks fight? They fought till they were all bloody, and almost blind. How foolish were they to fight and hurt each other so! They got no good by fighting; but they got sadly hurt. So boys get no good by quarrelling, but much hurt.

3. Do you see the dogs fight? Foolish dogs, how they bite one another! they are all bloody, as the fighting cocks were. See! one of them has got his ear almost bit off. I am sure they get no good by fighting; they had much better live in peace like good dogs, and be friendly to each other.

4. Look at the lambs in the field, how innocent they are; how they skip about and play; they do not quarrel and hurt one another, like the foolish dogs. Sweet lambs! how prettily do they play together; and so do good boys and girls.

5. So do the little kittens play together; they jump and run about the floor, and try a thousand merry tricks, but they do not quarrel; and how shameful it is for boys to quarrel!

Let dogs delight to bark and bite,
  For God hath made them so:
Let bears and lions growl and fight,
  For 'tis their nature too.
But children, you should never let
  Such angry passions rise;
Your little hands were never made
  To tear each other's eyes.

CHAPTER XLVIII. FORTY-EIGHTH.

A MORNING HYMN.

Lord! in the morning Thou shalt hear
  My voice ascending high!
To thee will I direct my prayer,
  To thee lift up mine eye.

Thou art a God before whose sight
  The wicked shall not stand:
Sinners shall ne'er be thy delight,
  Nor dwell at thy right hand.

But to thy house will I resort,
  To taste thy mercies there;
I will frequent thine holy court,
  And worship in thy fear.

O may thy spirit guide my feet,
  In ways of righteousness!
Make every path of duty straight,
  And plain before my face.

AN EVENING HYMN.

Lord! thou wilt hear me when I pray
  I am for ever thine;
I fear before thee all the day,
  Nor would I dare to sin.

And while I rest my weary head,
  From care and bus'ness free,
Tis sweet conversing on my bed
  With my own heart and Thee.

I pay this evening sacrifice,
  And when my work is done,
Great God, my faith and hope relies
  Upon thy grace alone.

Thus with my thoughts composed,
  I give mine eyes to sleep;
Thy hand in safety keeps my days,
  And will my slumbers keep.

ADVICE TO CHILDREN.

Children! to your Creator, God,
  Your early honors pay:
While vanity and youthful blood
  Would tempt your feet astray.

The memory of his mighty name,
  Demands your first regard;
Nor dare indulge a meaner flame,
  Till you have loved the Lord.

Be wise, and make his favor sure,
  Before the mournful days,
When youth and mirth are known no more,
  And life and strength decays.

No more the blessings of a feast
  Shall relish on your tongue;
The heavy ear forgets the taste
  And pleasure of a song.

Old age, with all her dismal train,
  Invades your golden years
With sighs, and groans, and raging pain,
  And death that never spares.

What will you do when life departs,
  And leaves your withering eyes,
Without one beam to cheer your hearts,
  From the superior skies?

The bands of nature soon will burst,
  And let the building fall;
Your flesh must mingle with the dust,
  Its vile original.

Laden with guilt, a heavy load,
  Uncleans'd and unforgiven,
The soul would fain ascend to God,
  But is shut out of heaven.

CHAPTER XLIX. FORTY-NINTH.

ODE TO CHILDHOOD!

Childhood! happiest stage of life,
Free from care, and free from strife;
Free from mem'ry's ruthless reign,
Fraught with scenes of former pain;
Free from fancy's cruel skill,
Fabricating future ill:
Time when all that meets the view,
All can charm, for all is new;
How thy long-lost hours I mourn,
Never, never, to return!
Then to toss the circling ball,
Caught rebounding from the wall;
Then the mimic ship to guide
Down the kennel's dirty tide;
Then the hoop's revolving pace
Through the dusty streets to chase;
Oh, what joy! it once was mine;
Childhood! matchless boon of thine:

How thy long-lost hours I mourn,
Never, never, to return!

TRUE RICHES.

I am not concern'd to know,
What to-morrow's fate will do:
'Tis enough that I can say,
I possess myself to-day—
Glitt'ring stones and golden things,
Wealth and honor, that have wings,
Ever flutt'ring to be gone,
I could never call my own.
Riches that the world bestows,
She can take, and I can lose;
But the treasures that are mine,
Lie afar beyond her line:
When I view my spacious soul,
And survey myself a whole;
And enjoy myself alone,
I'm a kingdom of my own.

THE DYING CHRISTIAN TO HIS SOUL.

Vital spark of heavenly flame;
Quit, oh quit this mortal frame;
Trembling, hoping, ling'ring, flying;
Oh, the pain, the bliss of dying;
Cease, fond nature, cease thy strife,
And let me languish into life.
Hark! They whisper: angels say,
"Sister spirit, come away."
What is this absorbs me quite!
Steals my senses, shuts my sight;
Drowns my spirits, draws my breath!
Tell me, my soul, can this be death?

The world recedes, it disappears;
Heaven opens on my eyes, my ears
With sounds seraphic ring;
Lend, lend your wings! I mount, I fly!
O grave, where is thy victory?
O Death, where is thy sting?

CHAPTER L. FIFTIETH.

ADVICE TO YOUTH.

Now, in the heat of youthful blood,
Remember your Creator, God;
Behold the months come hast'ning on,
When you shall say, " My joys are gone."
Behold the aged sinner goes
Laden with guilt and heavy woes,
Down to the regions of the dead,
With endless curses on his head.
Eternal King, I fear thy name,
Teach me to know how frail I am;
And when my soul must hence remove,
Give me a mansion in thy love.

ON THE SHORTNESS OF HUMAN LIFE.

Like as a damask rose you see,
Or like the blossom on the tree:
Or like the dainty flower of May,
Or like the morning to the day:
Or like the sun, or like the shade;
Or like the gourd which Jonas had:
Even such is man! whose thread is spun,
Drawn out, and cut, and so 'tis done.
Withers the rose, the blossom blasts;
The flower fades, the morning hastes;

The sun is set, the shadows fly:
The gourd consumes—so mortals die.

ONE OF SOLOMON'S SONGS.

The voice of my beloved sounds,
While o'er the mountain-top he bounds;
He flies exulting o'er the hills,
And all my soul with transport fills.
  Gently doth he chide my stay,
  Rise up my love, and come away.

The scatter'd clouds are fled at last,
The rain is gone, the winter past;
The lovely vernal flowers appear,
The warbling choir enchants the ear.
  Now with sweetly-pensive moan,
  Cooes the turtle-dove alone.

CHAPTER LI. FIFTY-FIRST.

EMMA.

Ye shepherds! she's fair as the light,
  The critic no blemish can find:
While all the soft VIRTUES unite,
  And glow in her innocent mind.

Her accents are fitted to please,
  Her manners engagingly free;
Her temper is ever at ease,
  And calm as an angel can be.

Her presence all sorrow removes,
  She enraptures the wit and the clown,
Her heart is as mild as the dove's,
  Her hand is as soft as its down.

Yon lily which graces the field,
And throws its perfume on the gale,
In fairness and fragrance must yield
To Emma, the pride of the vale.

She 's pleasant as yonder cool rill,
To trav'lers who faint on the way:
She 's sweet as the rose on the hill,
When it opens its bosom to day.

I ask not for wealth, nor for power:
Kind heaven! I these can resign;
But hasten, O hasten the hour,
When Emma shall deign to be mine.

CHAPTER LII. FIFTY-SECOND.

A Pastoral Ballad, in four Parts.—Shenstone

1.—ABSENCE.

Ye shepherds so cheerful and gay,
Whose flocks never carelessly roam:
Should Corydon's happen to stray,
O call the poor wanderers home.

Allow me to muse and to sigh,
  Nor talk of the change that ye find;
None once was so watchful as I:
  I have left my dear Phyllis behind.

Now I know what it is to have strove
  With the torture of doubt and desire;
What it is to admire and to love,
  And to leave her we love and admire.

Ah, lead forth my flock in the morn,
  And the damps of each evening repel:
Alas! I am faint and forlorn:
  I have bade my dear Phyllis farewell.

Since Phyllis vouchsafed me a look,
  I never once dream'd of my vine;
May I lose both my pipe and my crook,
  If I knew of a kid that was mine.

I prized every hour that went by,
  Beyond all that had pleased me before;
But now they are pass'd, and I sigh,
  And I grieve that I prized them no more.

But why do I languish in vain?
  Why wander thus pensively here?
O, why did I come from the plain,
  Where I fed on the smiles of my dear?

They tell me, my favorite maid,
  The pride of that valley, is flown:
Alas! where with her I have stray'd,
  I could wander with pleasure, alone.

When forc'd the fair nymph to forego,
  What anguish I felt at my heart!
Yet I thought—that it might not be so—
  'Twas with pain that she saw me depart.

She gazed as I slowly withdrew;
  My path I could hardly discern;

So sweetly she bade me adieu,
I thought that she bade me return.

The pilgrim that journeys all day,
To visit some far-distant shrine,
If he bear but a relic away,
Is happy, nor heard to repine.

Thus, widely removed from the fair,
Where my vows, my devotion, I owe,
Soft hope is the relic I bear,
And my solace wherever I go.

2.—HOPE.

My banks they are furnish'd with bees,
Whose murmur invites one to sleep;
My grottoes are shaded with trees,
And my hills are white over with sheep.

I seldom have met with a loss,
Such health do my fountains bestow;
My fountains all border'd with moss,
Where the hare-bells and violets grow.

Not a pine in my grove is there seen,
But with tendrils of woodbine is bound;
Not a beech's more beautiful green,
But a sweet-brier twines it around.

Not my fields in the prime of the year,
More charms than my cattle unfold;
Not a brook that is limpid and clear,
But it glitters with fishes of gold.

One would think she might like to retire
To the bow'r I have labor'd to rear;
Not a shrub that I heard her admire,
But I hasted and planted it there.

O how sudden the jessamine strove
  With the lilac, to render it gay!
Already it calls for my love,
  To prune the wild branches away.

From the plains, from the woodlands, and groves,
  What strains of wild melody flow!
How the nightingales warble their loves,
  From the thickets of roses that blow!

And when her bright form shall appear,
  Each bird shall harmoniously join
In a concert so soft and so clear,
  As—she may not be fond to resign.

I have found out a gift for my fair,
  I have found where the wood-pigeons breed,
But let me that plunder forbear,
  She will say 'twas a barbarous deed.

For he ne'er could be true, she averr'd,
  Who could rob a poor bird of its young;
And I lov'd her the more, when I heard
  Such tenderness fall from her tongue.

I have heard her with sweetness unfold,
  How that pity was due to a dove;
That it ever attended the bold,
  And she call'd it the sister of love.

But her words such a pleasure convey,
  So much I her accents adore,
Let her speak, and, whatever she say,
  Methinks I should love her the more.

Can a bosom so gentle remain
  Unmov'd, when her Corydon sighs?
Will a nymph that is fond of the plain
  These plains and this valley despise?

Dear regions of silence and shade!
  Soft scenes of contentment and ease!

Where I could have pleasingly stray'd,
  If aught in her absence could please.

But where does my Philida stray?
  And where are her grots and her bowers?
Are the groves and the valleys as gay,
  And the shepherds as gentle as ours?

Their groves may perhaps be as fair,
  And the face of the valleys as fine,
The swains may in manners compare,
  But their love is not equal to mine.

3.—SOLICITUDE.

Why will you my passion reprove?
  Why term it a folly to grieve,
Ere I show you the charms of my love?
  She is fairer than you can believe.

With her mien she enamours the brave;
  With her wit she engages the free;
With her modesty, pleases the grave;
  She's every way pleasing to me.

O you that have been of her train,
  Come and join in my amorous lays!
I could lay down my life for the swain
  That will sing but a song in her praise.

When he sings, may the nymphs of the town
  Come trooping, and listen the while;
Nay, on him let not Philida frown:
  But I cannot allow her to smile.

For when Paridel tries in the dance
  Any favor with Phyllis to find,
O how, with one trivial glance,
  Might she ruin the peace of my mind!

In ringlets he dresses his hair,
  And his crook is bestudded around;
And his pipe—O may Phyllis beware
  Of a magic there is in the sound!

'Tis his with mock passions to glow;
  'Tis his in smooth tales to unfold,
" How her face is as bright as the snow,
  And her bosom, be sure, is as cold:

How the nightingales labor the strain,
  With the notes of his charmer to vie;
How they vary their accents in vain,
  Repine at her triumphs, and die."

To the grove or the garden he strays,
  And pillages every sweet;
Then suiting the wreath to his lays,
  He throws it at Phyllis's feet.

" O Phyllis," he whispers, " more fair,
  More sweet than the jessamine's flower!
What are pinks, in a morn, to compare?
  What is eglantine after a shower?

Then the lily no longer is white;
  Then the rose is depriv'd of its bloom
Then the violets die with despite,
  And the woodbines give up their perfume."

Thus glide the soft numbers along,
  And he fancies no shepherd his peer;
Yet I never should envy the song,
  Were not Phyllis to lend it an ear.

Let his crook be with hyacinths bound,
  So Phyllis the trophy despise;
Let his forehead with laurels be crown'd,
  So they shine not in Phyllis's eyes.

The language that flows from the heart,
  Is a stranger to Paridel's tongue;
Yet may she beware of his art,
  Or sure I must envy the song.

4.—DISAPPOINTMENT.

Ye shepherds, give ear to my lay,
  And take no more heed of my sheep:
They have nothing to do but to stray,
  I have nothing to do but to weep.

Yet do not my folly reprove:
  She was fair—and my passion begun
She smil'd—and I could not but love;
  She is faithless—and I am undone.

Perhaps I was void of all thought;
  Perhaps it was plain to foresee
That a nymph so complete would be sought
  By a swain more engaging than me.

Ah! love every hope can inspire:
  It banishes wisdom the while;
And the lip of the nymph we admire
  Seems for ever adorn'd with a smile!

She is faithless, and I am undone;
  Ye that witness the woes I endure,
Let reason instruct you to shun
  What it cannot instruct you to cure.

Beware how you loiter in vain
  Amid nymphs of a higher degree:
It is not for me to explain
  How fair, and how fickle, they be.

Alas! from the day that we met,
  What hope of an end to my woes,
When I cannot endure to forget
  The glance that undid my repose?

Yet time may diminish the pain;
  The flow'r, and the shrub, and the tree,
Which I rear'd for her pleasure in vain,
  In time may have comfort for me.

The sweets of a dew-sprinkled rose,
  The sound of a murmuring stream,
The peace which from solitude flows,
  Henceforth shall be Corydon's theme.

High transports are shown to the sight,
  But we are not to find them our own;
Fate never bestow'd such delight,
  As I with my Phyllis had known.

O ye woods, spread your branches apace;
  To your deepest recesses I fly:
I would hide with the beasts of the chase,
  I would vanish from every eye.

Yet my reed shall resound through the grove,
  With the same sad complaint it begun;
How she smil'd, and I could not but love;
  Was faithless, and I am undone!

TO A REDBREAST.

Little bird, with bosom red,
Welcome to my humble shed!
Daily near my table steal,
While I pick my scanty meal.
Doubt not, little though there be,
That I'll cast a crumb to thee:
Well rewarded, if I spy
Pleasure in thy glancing eye;
See thee, when thou'st eat thy fill,
Plume thy breast and wipe thy bill.
Come, my feather'd friend, again!
Well thou know'st the broken pane.
Ask of me thy daily store;
Ever welcome to my door!

CHAPTER LIII. FIFTY-THIRD.

THE SEASONS.

SPRING.

Ah! see how the ice is all melting away,
The rivers have burst from their chain;
The woods and the hedges with verdure look gay,
And daisies enamel the plain.

The sun rises high and shines warm o'er the dale,
The orchards with blossoms are white:
The voice of the wood-lark is heard in the vale,
And the cuckoo returns from her flight.

Young lambs sport and frisk on the sides of the hill,
The honey-bee wakes from her sleep,
The turtle-dove opens her soft cooing bill,
And snow-drops and primroses peep.

All nature looks active, delightful, and gay,
  The creatures begin their employ;
Ah! let me not be less industrious than they,
  An idle, or indolent boy.

Now, while in the spring of my vigor and bloom,
  In the paths of fair learning I'll run;
Nor let the best part of my being consume,
  With nothing of consequence done.

Thus while to my lessons with care I attend,
  And store up the knowledge I gain,
When the winter of age shall upon me descend,
  'Twill cheer the dark season of pain.

SUMMER.

The heats of the summer come hastily on,
  The fruits are transparent and clear;
The buds and the blossoms of April are gone,
  And the deep-color'd cherries appear.

The blue sky above is bright and serene,
  No cloud on its bosom remains;
The woods and the fields, and the hedges, are green,
  And the hay-cock smells sweet from the plains.

Down in the fair valley where bubbles the spring,
  Which soft through the meadow-land glides,
The lads from the mountain the heavy sheep bring,
  And shear the warm coat from their sides.

Ah! let me lie down in some shady retreat,
  Beside the meandering stream,
For the sun darts abroad an intolerable heat,
  And burns with his overhead beam.

There all the day idle, my limbs I'll extend,
  Fann'd soft to delicious repose;
While round me a thousand sweet odors ascend,
  From ev'ry gay wood-flower that blows.

But hark, from the lowlands what sounds do I hear,
  The voices of pleasure so gay;
The merry young hay-makers cheerfully bear
  The heat of the hot summer's day.

While some with the scythe, singing shrill to the stone,
  The tall grass and butter-weeds mow,
Some spread it with rakes, and by others 'tis thrown
  Into sweet-smelling cocks in a row.

Then since joy and glee with activity join,
  This moment to labor I'll rise;
While the idle love best in the shade to recline,
  And waste precious time as it flies.

To waste precious time we can never recall,
  Is waste of the wickedest kind;
An instant of life has more value than all
  The gold that in India they find.

Not di'monds that brilliantly beam in the mine,
  For one moment's time should be given;
For gems can but make us look gaudy and fine,
  But time can prepare us for heaven.

AUTUMN.

The sun is far risen above the old trees,
  His beams on the silver dew play;
The gossamer tenderly waves in the breeze,
  And the mists are fast rolling away.

Let us leave the warm bed and the pillow of down,
  The morning fair bids us arise,
Little boy—for the shadows of midnight are flown,
  And sunbeams peep into our eyes.

We'll pass by the garden that leads to the gate,
  But where is its gaiety now?
The Michaelmas daisy blows lonely and late,
  And the yellow leaf whirls from the bough.

Last night the glad reapers their harvest-home sung,
And stor'd the full garners with grain;
Did you hear how the woods with their merry shouts rung,
As they bore the last sheaf from the plain?

But hark! from the woodlands the sound of a gun!
The wounded bird flutters and dies:
Ah! surely 'tis wicked for nothing but fun
To shoot the poor thing as it flies.

The timid hare too, in affright and dismay,
Runs swift through the brush-wood and grass;
How she turns, how she winds, and tries every way
But the cruel dogs won't let her pass.

Ah! poor little partridge, and pheasant, and hare,
I wish they would leave you to live;
For my part, I wonder how people can bear
To see all the torment they give.

When Reynard, at midnight, steals down to the farm
And kills the poor chickens and cocks;
Then rise farmer Goodman, there can be no harm
In killing a thief of a fox.

But the innocent hare, and the pheasant so sleek,
'Twere cruel and wicked to slay:
The partridge, with blood never redden'd her beak,
Nor hares stole the poultry away.

If folks would but think of the torture they give,
To creatures who cannot complain;
I think they would let the poor animals live,
Nor ever go shooting again.

WINTER.

Behold the gray branches that stretch from the trees,
  Nor blossom nor verdure they wear!
They rattle and shake to the northerly breeze,
  And wave their long arms in the air.

The sun hides his face in a mantle of clouds,
  Dark vapors roll over the sky!
The wind through the woods hollows hoarsely and loud,
  And sea-birds across the land fly.

Come in, little Charles, for the snow patters down,
  No paths in the garden remain;
The streets and the houses are white in the town,
  And white are the fields and the plain.

Como in, little Charles, from the tempest of snow,
  'Tis dark, and the shutters we'll close:
We'll put a fresh fagot to make the fire glow,
  Secure from the storm as it blows.

But how many wretches, without house or home,
Are wandering naked and pale:
Obliged on the snow-cover'd common to roam,
And pierced by the pitiless gale;

No house for their shelter, no victuals to eat,
No bed for their limbs to repose:
Or their crust, dry and mouldy, the best of their meat
And their pillow, a pillow of snows.

Be thankful, my child, that it is not your lot,
To wander, an orphan, and poor;
A father, and mother, and home, you have got,
And yet you deserved them no more.

Be thankful my child, and forget not to pray,
Give thanks to that Father above,
Who gives you so many more blessings than they,
And crowns your whole life with his love.

Ode from the 19*th Psalm.*

The spacious firmament on high,
With all the blue ethereal sky,
And spangled heavens, a shining frame,
Their great Original proclaim.
Th' unwearied sun, from day to day,
Does his Creator's power display:
And publishes to ev'ry land,
The work of an Almighty hand.

Soon as the evening shades prevail,
The moon takes up the wondrous tale,
And, nightly, to the list'ning earth,
Repeats the story of her birth;
Whilst all the stars that round her burn,
And all the planets in their turn,
Confirm the tidings as they roll,
And spread the truth from pole to pole.

What though in solemn silence, all
Move round the dark terrestrial ball?
What though no real voice nor sound
Amid these radiant orbs be found?
In reason's ear they all rejoice,
And utter forth a glorious voice,
For ever singing, as they shine,
"The hand that made us is divine."

THE IDLE BOY.

Thomas was an idle lad,
And lounged about all day;
And though he many a lesson had,
He minded nought but play.

He only cared for top or ball,
Or marbles, hoop, and kite;
But as for learning, that was all
Neglected by him, quite.

In vain his mother's kind advice,
In vain his master's care,
He follow'd ev'ry idle vice,
And learnt to curse and swear!

And think you, when he grew a man,
He prosper'd in his ways?
No,—wicked courses never can
Bring good and happy days.

Without a shilling in his purse,
Or cot to call his own,
Poor Thomas grew from bad to worse,
And harden'd as a stone.

And oh, it grieves me much to write
His melancholy end,
Then let us leave the dreadful sight,
And thoughts of pity send.

But may we this important truth,
  Observe and ever hold,
"All those who're idle in their youth,
  Will suffer when they're old."

CHAPTER LIV. FIFTY-FOURTH.

FRIENDSHIP.

The world, my dear Myra, is full of deceit,
And friendship's a jewel we seldom can meet;
How strange does it seem that in searching around,
This source of delight is so rare to be found!
O FRIENDSHIP! thou balm and rich sweet'ner of life,
Kind parent of ease, and composer of strife:
Without Thee, alas! what are riches and power,
But empty delusion, the joys of an hour!
How much to be priz'd, and esteem'd, is a friend,
On whom we may always with safety depend;
Our joys, when extended, will always increase,
And griefs, when divided, are hush'd into peace.
When fortune is smiling, whole crowds will appear,
Their kindness to offer, and friendship sincere;
Yet change but the prospect, and point out distress,
No longer to court you, they eagerly press.

COLUMBIA.

Fair Science her gates to thy sons shall unbar,
And the east see thy morn hide the beams of her star;
New bards and new ages unrivall'd shall soar
To fame unextinguish'd, till time be no more;
To thee, the last refuge of virtue design'd,
Shall fly from all nations, the best of mankind;
Here, grateful to Heaven, with transport shall bring,
Their incense, more fragrant than odors of spring.

Nor less shall thy fair ones to glory ascend,
And genius and beauty in harmony blend;
The graces of form shall awake pure desire,
And the charms of the soul still enliven the fire:
Their sweetness unmingled, their manners refin'd,
And virtue's bright image impress'd on the mind,
With peace and soft rapture shall teach life to glow,
And light up a smile in the bosom of woe.

CHAPTER LV. FIFTY-FIFTH.

PEACE.

Hail! sacred Peace, who claim'st thy bright abode
'Mid circling saints that grace the throne of God;
Ere morning stars his glowing chambers hung,
Or songs of gladness woke an angel's tongue;
Veil'd in the brightness of the Almighty's mind,
In blest repose thy placid form reclin'd;
Borne through the heaven, with his creating voice,
Thy presence bade the unfolding worlds rejoice,
Gave to seraphic harps their sounding lays,
Their joys to angels, and to men their praise.
Bring, bounteous Peace, in thy celestial throng,
Life to my soul, and rapture to my song;
Give me to trace, with pure unclouded ray,
The arts and virtues that attend thy sway;
To see thy blissful charms, that here descend,
Through distant realms and endless years extend

THE WAY TO BE HAPPY.

How pleasant it is, at the end of the day,
  No follies to have to repent,
But reflect on the past, and be able to say,
  That my time has been properly spent!

When I've done all my bus'ness with patience and care,
And been good, and obliging, and kind,
I lay on my pillow, and sleep away there,
With a happy and peaceable mind.

But instead of all this, if it must be confess'd,
That I careless and idle have been;
I lay down as usual and go to my rest,
But feel discontented within.

Then, as I don't like all the trouble I've had,
In future I'll try to prevent it;
For I never am naughty without being sad,
Or good—without being contented.

THE FOX AND THE CROW.

The fox and the crow,
In prose, I well know,
Many good little girls can rehearse;
Perhaps it will tell
Pretty nearly as well,
If we try the same fable in verse.

In a dairy a crow
Having ventured to go,
Some food for her young ones to seek,
Flew up in the trees
With a fine piece of cheese,
Which she joyfully held in her beak.

A fox who lived nigh,
To the tree saw her fly,
And to share in the prize made a vow:
For having just dined,
He for cheese felt inclined,
So he went and sat under the bough.

She was cunning he knew,
But so was he too,
And with flatt'ry adopted his plan;
For he knew if she'd speak,
It must fall from her beak,
So, bowing politely, began:

"'Tis a very fine day;
(Not a word did she say;)
The wind, I believe, ma'am, is south;
A fine harvest for peas:"
He then looked at the cheese,
But the crow did not open her mouth.

Sly Reynard, not tired,
Her plumage admired,
"How charming! how brilliant its hue!
The voice must be fine,
Of a bird so divine,
Ah! let me just hear it—pray do.

Believe me, I long
To hear a sweet song."
The silly crow foolishly tries.—
She scarce gave one squall,
When the cheese she let fall,
And the fox ran away with the prize.

MORAL.

Ye innocent fair,
Of coxcombs beware,
To flattery never give ear;
Try well each pretence,
And keep to plain sense,
And then you have little to fear.

M

CHAPTER LVI. FIFTY-SIXTH.

THE NIGHTINGALE AND THE GLOW-WORM.

A nightingale, that all day long
Had cheer'd the village with his song,
Nor yet at eve his note suspended,
Nor yet when eventide was ended,
Began to feel, as well he might,
The keen demands of appetite;
When, looking eagerly around,
He spied far off, upon the ground,
A something shining in the dark,
And knew the glow-worm by his spark;
So, stooping down from hawthorn top,
He thought to put him in his crop.

The worm, aware of his intent,
Harangued him thus, right eloquent—
"Did you admire my lamp," quoth he,
"As much as I your minstrelsy,
You would abhor to do me wrong,
As much as I to spoil your song;
For 'twas the self-same Power divine,
Taught you to sing, and me to shine;
That you with music, I with light,
Might beautify and cheer the night."

The songster heard his short oration,
And, warbling out his approbation,
Releas'd him, as my story tells,
And found a supper somewhere else.
Hence, jarring sectaries may learn
Their real int'rest to discern;
That brother should not war with brother,
And worry and devour each other:
But sing and shine by sweet consent,
Till life's poor, transient night is spent:

Respecting, in each other's case,
The gifts of nature and of grace.

Those Christians best deserve the name,
Who studiously make peace their aim:
Peace, both the duty and the prize
Of him that creeps, and him that flies.

A MORNING IN SPRING.

Lo! the bright, the rosy morning,
  Calls me forth to take the air:
Cheerful spring, with smiles returning,
  Ushers in the new-born year.

Nature now in all her beauty,
  With her gently-moving tongue,
Prompts me to the pleasing duty
  Of a grateful morning song.

See the early blossoms springing!
  See the jocund lambkins play!
Hear the lark and linnet singing,
  Welcome to the new-born day!

Vernal music, softly sounding,
  Echoes through the verdant grove:
Nature now, with life abounding,
  Swells with harmony and love.

Now the kind refreshing showers
  Water all the plains around:
Springing grass, and painted flowers,
  In the smiling meads abound.

Now, their vernal dress assuming,
  Leafy robes adorn the trees:
Odors now, the air perfuming,
  Sweetly swell the gentle breeze.

Praise to thee, thou great Creator!
  Praise be thine from ev'ry tongue
Join, my soul, with ev'ry creature;
  Join the universal song!

For ten thousand blessings giv'n;
  For the richest gifts bestow'd;
Sound his praise through earth and heav'n;
  Sound Jehovah's praise aloud!

ON EARLY RISING.

How foolish they who lengthen night,
And slumber in the morning light!
How sweet, at early morning's rise,
To view the glories of the skies,
And mark with curious eye the sun
Prepare his radiant course to run!
Its fairest form then nature wears,
And clad in brightest green appears.
The sprightly lark, with artless lay,
Proclaims the entrance of the day.

How sweet to breathe the gale's perfume,
And feast the eye with nature's bloom!
Along the dewy lawn to rove,
And hear the music of the grove!
Nor you, ye delicate and fair,
Neglect to taste the morning air;
This will your nerves with vigor brace,
Improve and heighten ev'ry grace;
Add to your breath a rich perfume;
Add to your cheeks a fairer bloom:
With lustre teach your eyes to glow;
And health and cheerfulness bestow.

THE DROWNING FLY.

In yonder glass behold a drowning fly!
Its little feet, how vainly does it ply!
Poor helpless insect! and will no one save?
Will no one snatch thee from the threat'ning grave?
My finger's top shall prove a friendly shore.—
There, trembler, all thy dangers now are o'er.
Wipe thy wet wings, and banish all thy fear:
Go, join thy numerous kindred in the air.
Away it flies; resumes its harmless play;
And lightly gambols in the golden ray.

Smile not, spectators, at this humble deed:
For you, perhaps, a nobler task 's decreed:
A young and sinking family to save;
To raise the thoughtless from destruction's wave
To you, for help, the wretched lift their eyes:
Oh! hear, for pity's sake, their plaintive cries:
Ere long, unless some guardian interpose,
O'er their devoted heads, the floods may close.

A PRAYER.

Father of light and life, Thou good supreme!
O teach me what is good! teach me thyself!
Save me from folly, vanity, and vice:
From every low pursuit: and fill my soul
With knowledge, conscious peace, and virtue pure,
Sacred, substantial, never-fading bliss.

THE LORD'S PRAYER.

Our Father which art in heaven, hallowed be thy name. Thy kingdom come. Thy will be done in earth as *it is* in heaven: give us this day our daily bread; and forgive us our debts, as we forgive our debtors. And lead us not into temptation, but deliver us from evil. For thine is the kingdom, and the power, and the glory, for ever. Amen.

THE TEN COMMANDMENTS IN VERSE.

1. No other God have thou than me,
2. Before no idol bow thy knee,
3. Take not the name of God in vain,
4. Nor dare the sabbath day profane.
5. Give both thy parents honor due,
6. Take heed that thou no murder do.
7. Abstain from words and deeds unclean,
8. Nor steal though thou art poor and mean,
9. Nor tell a wilful lie nor love it,
10. What is thy neighbors do not covet.

That unto others never fail to do,
Which you would have them do to you.

THE END.

www.ingramcontent.com/pod-product-compliance
Lightning Source LLC
LaVergne TN
LVHW021418110826
845150LV00007B/1979

* 9 7 8 1 4 2 5 5 0 9 7 7 4 *